Invitation
to the
New Testament

Invitation to the New Testament

A Catholic Approach to the Christian Scriptures

Alice Camille

ACTA

ASSISTING CHRISTIANS TO ACT

PUBLICATIONS

Invitation to the New Testament
A Catholic Approach to the Christian Scriptures
by Alice Camille

Editing by Kass Dotterweich
Cover design by Tom A. Wright
Cover art by Jean Morman Unsworth
Typesetting by Desktop Edit Shop, Inc.

Published by: ACTA Publications
Assisting Christians To Act
4848 N. Clark Street
Chicago, IL 60640-4711
773-271-1030
www.actapublications.com

Library of Congress Catalog Number: 2004104884
ISBN: 0-87946-269-8
Printed in the United States of America
Year: 10 9 8 7 6 5 4
Printing: 7 6 5 4 3 2 1

Contents

Dedication

For my sister, Sue Showalter
who would follow Jesus to Kingdom Come

A Relationship with Jesus

"When you see Jesus coming," my sister Sue warns me, "*run* in the opposite direction!" We both laugh. Sue is a practicing Catholic and earnest about her faith. She is only half kidding, though, when she counsels me to avoid Jesus, because she knows from personal experience the high price of following him. She knows Jesus is not a fellow to be squeezed into your life, someone you can make time for between one activity and another (the way we often make time for church). A relationship with Jesus is a love affair: all-encompassing, passionate and demanding. After all, there is no such thing as a little bit of love and a small amount of commitment.

One ought to be clearly forewarned about this: If you choose to follow Jesus, your life will not be anything you expect or intend. Be prepared to surrender business-as-usual for something new and surprising. In fact, it is fair to suggest that those who want to hold on to the life they have and don't intend to change ought to stop going to church immediately!

This idea wasn't made clear to me all at once. I grew up in the generation of Catholics who were just beginning to absorb the message of the Second Vatican Council of the early 1960s and coming to understand that the "changes" happening in the Church were not merely cosmetic. The Church of my earliest recollections, to be honest, did not have a lot to say about Jesus. I remember hearing a lot about what God wanted and didn't want, liked and didn't like. I also heard a great deal about the Church, with a capital C, which at that time meant the hierarchy and most definitely didn't include the likes of me. I knew my place was to be obedient—to God and to the Church. Back then, the distinction between the two—God and the Church— did not seem important.

1

Parochial grade school didn't challenge that limited perspective, but attending Catholic high school certainly did. I was surprised that first year when Sister Maureen asked us to form teams to debate some religious issues. *Debate?* I didn't think Catholics were supposed to do that. Wasn't everything fixed in stone—or at least in papal encyclicals? Wasn't our job simply to memorize and follow through? Nonetheless, debating made me think seriously about these issues, which I eventually realized I'd never done before. Forced to research the positions Catholics held, I discovered the sources behind the authority. I began to understand that Church teaching didn't emerge in the mind of the pope each morning after breakfast. I grew to appreciate the fact that each teaching was rooted in—and sought to build on—the mind of Christ.

As ground-shaking as that first year of high school religion was, I was even more deeply affected as a sophomore, when Sister Denise Marie asked us to spend the year writing a Jesus journal. I'd been keeping a diary since the fourth grade, but this was different. She wanted a written dialogue between me and Jesus—a person I soon realized I hardly knew.

How were we to come to know this Jesus well enough to confide in him? Sister devised a host of ways. We read passages from the Gospels, of course, and we reflected on the sacraments and how they revealed Jesus to us. But we also looked at world events—like the Vietnam War and Watergate, believe it or not—for signs of how Jesus might be speaking to us. We examined culture: movies and television and music and trends. Most peculiar of all, we were invited to scout out Jesus in the events of our personal lives and relationships—and in the recesses of that fearful place, the teenage heart.

After spending a year in close communion with Jesus, doing something as far from praying as anything I'd ever done, I finally *got* it. Jesus was to be sought everywhere, in every aspect of our lives. If Jesus was to be real to us, and not some figment of the religious imagination, we had to take seriously his enduring presence. If following him is what we were supposed to be doing, he had to be our companion as well as our Lord. After a year of journaling, I was surprised to find that I no longer needed the notebook. Jesus and I, unexpectedly and vitally, had a relationship.

That may sound a little fishy. Beginning at the time of the Reformation five centuries ago, Catholics had grown more and more suspicious of anything that sounded "too Protestant"—and having a "personal relationship with Jesus" certainly rang the Protestant warning buzzer for me. Somewhere in the back of my mind, I had compartmentalized Christian ideals into two columns: "Catholic" and "Protestant." I had "sacraments" in the "Catholic" column and "Jesus as my personal savior" in the "Protestant" column. It would be tragic to think that in our efforts to preserve the sacramental worldview so dear to us, we Catholics might have unconsciously surrendered the person of Jesus, the one whom theologian Edward Schillebeeckx called "the sacrament of God." In its very definition, a sacrament is a channel or mediation of the holy, and it doesn't end with itself. Rather, it both reveals and conceals God for us. If we forfeit our relationship with Jesus in favor of the outward sign that represents him, we lose our pearl of great price.

Entering into an intimate relationship with Jesus, then, is critical for anyone who identifies himself or herself as Christian. Naturally, there is no one way to do this. Some of us, like Saint Paul, may be stopped on the road to Damascus (or Dayton or Dallas or Denver) and be personally confronted with the living Christ, so we may not have to go out of our way to begin such a relationship. In case your epiphany seems to be running late, however, there are plenty of variations on the Jesus journal idea that may help. Some people practice the ancient church prayer form known as *lectio divina* ("divine reading"). First you read aloud a passage from the Bible so that you can fully hear it and feel the words in your mouth. Then you enter into a silent dialogue with the passage, placing yourself in the scene as one of the characters or in conversation with Jesus directly. What would you say to him, and what would he say to you? Finally, you read the passage aloud again to see if it sounds different—now that you've "been there."

We can also practice turning over aspects of our lives to Jesus each day: certain troubling thoughts, relationships of con-

3

cern or conflict, health or financial worries, or tendencies that lead us into that old scenario known as "the near occasion of sin." Our relationship with Jesus is built the same way all of our relationships are built—gradually through time, shared company, increasing confidences, and the evolution of trust. But no friendship begins until we initiate that first real conversation. Jesus is here. The right time is now. All that's missing is our willingness to begin. Unlike some people we may know, Jesus is never pushy.

* * *

Anyone picking up this book presumably is already engaged in such a conversation with Jesus—or would like to be. That's what the New Testament is all about and why it was written. It's a conversation begun by the earliest followers of Jesus, and it ends in a question: Do you want to join us or don't you? It's not a collection of history books, and it's not a biography or a chronicle in the usual sense. Rather, the New Testament was written specifically for the purpose of evangelism—not journalism. It was written by the "convinced" for the sake of convincing others. For this reason, going to the New Testament won't give you the "facts" or the "evidence" in any scientific sense. Instead, it presents the journey, the testimony and the community of faith.

Do you want to come along or don't you? Are you in or are you out? As an appeal to decision, Christian Scripture cannot be read simply for its story line; it demands a response. Even if you say "no thank you," you have answered the question.

So what will you find in the New Testament? Centrally, it is the story of Jesus—you might say it makes the case for Jesus—told in four gospel accounts and other miscellaneous documents. It includes a book called the Acts of the Apostles, which is an account of the early Church in the first generation after the resurrection. Catholics of a certain age will remember the reading of the "epistles" at Mass, a fancy name for the letters written by early church giants such as Paul, John, James and Peter. Finally, thanks to a bath of pop exposure, just about everyone in this day and age knows that the Bible ends with a

4

strange and riveting document called the Book of Revelation or the Apocalypse.

Compared to the Old Testament, the New Testament is compact and manageable in many ways. Unlike Hebrew Scripture, which tells its story starting with the first act of creation and covers thousands of years of sprawling historical events and characters, the events chronicled in the New Testament are limited to one century and concentrate on two generations. The Old Testament was written over a period of about six hundred years (after untold generations of oral tradition) and had countless authors and schools involved in the shaping of its content. The New Testament was written in the space of fifty years and had a limited amount of oral and written transmission behind it. Hebrew Scripture has a cast worthy of Cecil B. De Mille, and one is compelled to make lists to keep the begetting straight. The New Testament has a handful of important characters who ferry us through the story with a clear sense of purpose and unshakeable direction. Where are they taking us so deliberately? Read on and see!

The intention of this book is to get into the skin of those early disciples and to come to an appreciation of what compelled the early Church to form the documents of the New Testament. We'll also look at heroes of that period, as well as conflicts that were present in the first community of Christians and—not surprisingly—may be found in our own communities today. We'll consider how each generation of the Church had a unique perspective on the gospel. And we'll examine how the Book of Revelation, strange as it seems, may be a "fifth gospel" of the New Testament.

Included with each chapter are questions for personal reflection or group use, as well as a suggested faith response to the ideas presented in the section. But the most important questions in this book are the ones the Evangelists of the New Testament are asking: Do you want to follow Jesus as the first disciples once did? Are you ready to make the testimony of the gospel your personal profession of faith? Are you prepared to join with this community and be *church?* Are you in...or are you out?

Writing Down the Story

What makes a good story such a fascination for us? Just think of the ocean of literature produced down through the ages in poetry, plays, histories and novels—not to mention the media of newspapers, magazines, radio, television, film and the Internet—that deliver stories to us regularly. Similarly, we narrate the ongoing saga of our lives, saving certain delicate stories for the privileged few and sharing others liberally with anyone who will listen. We are captivated by storytelling at an early age, and hunger for more all our lives.

What are we looking for in this constellation of tales? In some cases, we're looking for pure entertainment; in other instances, we're looking for instruction, insight, a sense of order, comfort, and maybe even meaning. Through our stories we communicate goals, values and a sense of identity. We even rate stories as "true," based on their correspondence to some historical moment in time as well as on how they manage to mirror universal experiences common to people in every age. True stories hold us together as families, communities, nations and religions. The best stories tell us who we are and where we are headed.

Because the vehicle of story has such a grip on our imagination and is such a powerful tool in forming our sense of self, we ought to consider taking responsibility for the stories we admit into our lives and repeat to others. Do we want to squander the power of story in reinforcing the oft-told tales of unrepentant greed, war, violence, dominance and deception? Or do we want to consider our diet of stories as seriously as we consider the foods we eat—recognizing that some are good for us while others consume our imagination without supplying anything of value, perhaps even doing us harm?

How the Gospels Came to Be Written

As we think about the nature and power of stories, we can understand why the story of Jesus was so important to those who had journeyed with him around Galilee and Judea. The experience of knowing Jesus had changed these people's lives. It turned everything they thought they knew upside down. Jesus' life, death and resurrection were such extraordinary experiences that his disciples felt compelled to tell the story. So they did, nonstop, for almost a generation. They preached in synagogues, shouted in town squares, and set up teaching engagements in people's homes. But something happened about thirty years after Jesus' resurrection that made writing down the story an absolute imperative. Perhaps you can guess what that event was: the death of the first Apostles. According to tradition, both Peter and Paul died in Rome as martyrs to the faith in the mid-sixties. Stephen, one of the first deacons, and James, John's brother, had already been killed; both deaths are recorded in the Acts of the Apostles. With the death of these eyewitnesses to the gospel events, who would be the bearers of this all-important story for the future?

Perhaps no one thought to write down the story before the 60s because many in the early Church took Jesus' promise to return (known as the *parousia* or Second Coming) as an event that could happen at any minute. There is no need to record a story for future generations if one is convinced there will be no future. But as that first generation of witnesses went to their deaths, the second generation of Church felt it advisable to start writing things down.

But what did these faithful followers of Jesus have to work with in order to do that? The first part of the New Testament to "go to print," so to speak, was the collection of Paul's letters. As you can see from a quick read through his writings, Paul was not concerned with telling the story of the life of Jesus to those with whom he corresponded. Paul or other missionaries would have shared those stories with the communities at the time they were founded. Paul also did not spend much space in his letters analyzing the teachings of Jesus or quoting his sayings—with the exception of the words spoken at the Last Supper,

8

known as "the words of institution" (see 1 Corinthians 11:23–26). For Paul, the actions of Jesus during his life were not as crucial as the significance of his suffering, death and resurrection. Who Jesus was revealed to be through those events— the *Christ* or "anointed one" of God—was the point of Christian faith. Paul, therefore, stuck to preaching "Jesus Christ, and him crucified" (1 Corinthians 2:2).

So we can see that Paul's letters would not be a useful resource for those intent on telling the story of Jesus. But scholars believe that there was some sort of "first" text that appeared before the Gospels we know about—a simple list of the popular sayings of Jesus that had been collected and written down. Those sayings would have formed the basis for the earliest attempts at telling the story of Jesus to others.

Gospel Order and the Story of Q

Nobody has a copy of the manuscript of Jesus' sayings that scholars refer to as Q. Short for the German word *quelle*, which means "source." Q is only a theory, but a pretty convincing one. Q was proposed as a result of centuries of debate about the order in which the Gospels were set down. If you look at your Bible, of course, there's no debate: the order is Matthew, Mark, Luke and John. But before there *was* a Bible, in which order did these stories emerge?

Rarely has anyone challenged that the fourth place belongs to John, a Gospel so obviously divergent from the rest. But the order of the first three was harder to establish because they are so similar. This trait earned Matthew, Mark and Luke the name *Synoptic* (meaning "the same") Gospels. Three texts so alike arguably could have appeared in any order.

The Gospels were arranged in the present order in the fourth century, when the *canon*, or authorized list, of inspired books was established for the New Testament. Some church fathers, like Clement of Alexandria (late second century), believed that the Gospel with genealogies should come first. Only Matthew and Luke included genealogies. Also, Matthew was the only Gospel attributed to an Apostle and eyewitness of the time of Jesus—so that cinched the case for placing him first.

The Gospels of Mark and Luke were both attributed to converts of Paul or Peter, according to the church fathers, so they were placed next. No one disputed that John's Gospel was written a generation after the first three. Because Saint Augustine—one of the great Doctors of the Church and an authority who wasn't to be crossed lightly—was in favor of the order familiar in our present Bible, the order he preferred stuck.

Few questioned this organization of the Gospels until the eighteenth century, when one biblical scholar advanced the theory that the correct order should be Matthew, Luke, Mark and John. Since Matthew and Luke both contain elements that show up in the Gospel of Mark, Mark must have had both texts in front of him when he wrote—or so the line of reasoning went. Because Mark was the shortest of the Synoptic Gospels (about half as long as Luke), this scholar saw Mark as an "extreme editor" who tried to condense and combine the other two traditions, removing any contradictory or singular aspects of the others from his version.

In the nineteenth century, this theory was basically reversed, and most scholars today believe that the Gospels were written in the following order: Mark, Matthew, Luke and John. It seems evident that the similarities in Matthew and Luke occur because *they* were copying from *Mark*, and not the other way around. Mark did not edit down existing versions; rather, those that came later added to his "standard" account. Still, Matthew and Luke share some stories in common that do not appear in Mark. So where did this shared-but-not-Mark material come from?

The answer is Q. Whatever Matthew and Luke have in common that is not from Mark must have come from another source familiar to both authors. No one has ever found a copy of Q, but if it turns up a lot of biblical scholars will be opening the champagne!

Mark: The First and the Shortest

But why should we care about the order of the Gospels? Well, for one thing, history is partial to the primary sources surrounding an event. Eyewitnesses count for more than hearsay.

10

The closer a piece of evidence is to the time and place about which it testifies, the more plausible and accurate it is considered to be. The first source, then, is often the most authoritative.

This doesn't mean that Mark's Gospel is better or truer than the others as a document of faith, but it may preserve a tad more historical acuity. If others used Mark in forming their own story, Mark becomes important not only for what he says but also for what he doesn't say. Which is another way of saying that if changes or additions were made in the later Gospels, those changes were deliberate departures from Mark's account. Uncovering the meaning behind the changes helps us to understand the perspective of later or parallel communities of Christians who produced or used these variant versions.

So for a moment let's approach Mark like detectives and see what we can learn about his Gospel. As noted, it's the shortest, a mere 661 verses compared to 1068 in Matthew and 1149 in Luke. Yet, ninety percent of what Mark wrote shows up in the other Synoptic Gospels, so clearly he was considered a very reliable source. Mark's brevity gives his story a breathless quality. Jesus and the disciples seem to hurry from town to town, doing as much teaching, healing and challenging as possible before turning to Jerusalem. The story is divided pretty evenly between two journeys: one through Galilee and the early ministry, which is quite successful; and the last journey toward Jerusalem and the final days.

Who was Mark? Authorship in the Bible is always a bit of a mystery. No one knows for certain who Mark was—the name gets affixed to the manuscript later, and internally the document claims only to be "the good news [gospel] of Jesus Christ, the Son of God" (1:1). The early church fathers identified the author with John Mark, a cousin of Barnabas and companion of Paul mentioned in Acts and several of Paul's letters. But a third-century church historian writes that in an earlier period Mark was recognized as Peter's co-worker, whom the first letter of Peter calls "my son Mark" (1 Peter 5:13). This historian noted that Mark had served as an interpreter for Peter and wrote down everything he remembered—although, he warns, not necessarily in order. Should we consider Mark a loose scribe for "the gospel according to Peter"?

Not all scholars are prepared to go that far. No internal evidence exists for the idea that Mark's Gospel is Peter's version of the story. However, scholars are fairly sure that this account was written before the year 70, since the Gospel doesn't allude to the devastating destruction of the Jerusalem Temple, which took place in that year—an event the other Gospels are certainly aware of. So we can date Mark roughly between 60 and 70. Don't bet the farm on those dates, however, as a new manuscript discovered tomorrow could lead to the next great theory.

Secrecy in Mark

Secrets are notoriously hard to keep. Privileged information regularly gets leaked—and often to the person you'd most like to keep it from. Calling something a "secret," in fact, is probably the best way to get the word out. Maybe that's why Mark used the device of the "secret" to withhold—and thereby announce —who Jesus really is.

When it comes right down to it, you could say that Mark invented the literary form known as the "gospel," so he gets to make the rules, and his first decision is to tell us at the start that Jesus Christ is the Son of God. But he follows that announcement by spending the rest of the story keeping that identity hidden in a stage-whispery sort of way. The Gospel seems organized around the keeping of this messianic secret: the mystery that Jesus is the Christ, the Messiah of God.

How does Mark keep us on the edge of this mystery? He brings it up in healing stories, as Jesus charges the healed leper or the formerly blind man not to tell anyone what has happened—as if they could hide it! Jesus also shouts down the demons who seek to announce him in every exorcism "because they knew him" (1:34, 3:12), forcing them to be silent. Jesus even goes so far as to tell the astonished parents of the girl he raises from the dead "that no one should know this" (5:43). After Peter acknowledges Jesus as the Messiah, Jesus warns the disciples not to tell anyone about him.

Needless to say, the more Jesus orders people not to speak

of what they see, the more they proclaim it. Is Jesus employing a first-century version of reverse-psychology on the crowds, or is Mark using it on his readers?

Certainly the identity of Jesus is a big theme—we might say the controlling theme—in Mark's story. From the time John the Baptist announces that "the one who is more powerful than I is coming" (1:7), we have great expectations. Jesus will be known by many names in this Gospel. To the voice from heaven that speaks at his baptism, he is the Beloved Son. His disciples call him Teacher. The demons shriek that he is the Son of the Most High God. To those who long for his help, he is a Son of David. The crowds identify him as a reincarnation of John the Baptist, Elijah, or one of the prophets, although to his enemies he is an agent of the prince of demons, possessed by an unclean spirit. His relatives think he's crazy and try to drag him home. Yet when Jesus speaks of himself, he uses the simple title Son of Man, which identifies him as one of us.

Perhaps one of the unkindest things Jesus was called, ironically, is "son of Mary" (6:3). This happens when he is rejected from his boyhood town of Nazareth. Elsewhere in the Bible, people are known in relationship to their fathers: David is the son of Jesse, and Peter is called Simon *bar* ("son of") Jonah. And then there is Barabbas, or Bar Abbas, literally "son of the father," perhaps implying "chip off the old block." Sad to say, an identification with your mother was most likely intended as an insult, a suggestion that your father's paternity is suspect. In Jesus' case, we can imagine such rumors haunted the family.

The identity of Jesus remains a critical theme throughout Mark's Gospel. When rescued from the storm on the lake, his astonished disciples ask, "Who then is this, that even the wind and the sea obey him?" (4:41) It was a question everyone was asking. And Mark saves his best answer for last. At the foot of the cross, a centurion, who is neither Jewish nor a disciple, watches the way Jesus dies and declares, "Truly this man was God's Son!" (15:39) Mark makes two things clear in this declaration. First is that the true identity of Jesus cannot be known apart from the cross. The second is a forecast: Those who see Jesus most clearly may be the ones who come to him most belatedly—the Gentiles.

Left Unsaid

Mark leaves much unspoken in his Gospel. He starts with the ministry of John the Baptist, so there is no Christmas story to fill in the blanks about Jesus' beginnings. In many of the earliest existing manuscripts of Mark, there is no explicit resurrection story at the end. Rather, the Gospel ends at 16:8, as the women discover the empty tomb. There they meet an angel who proclaims that Jesus has been raised—and promptly they run away. This time, frustratingly, Jesus' disciples say nothing to anyone because they are afraid. For once, they keep the secret—just when it's time to give it away!

Later editors added various longer endings to compensate for what seemed lacking in this awkward finish to Mark's Gospel. Compared with the other Synoptics, Mark certainly appears sliced off at both ends. But it's possible that Mark intended the Gospel to begin in the midst of the action and end with awkward silence—because, after all, don't we all come to this story in the midst of our lives and plans, and aren't we all confronted with the same information that the first disciples had? We come to the empty tomb and receive the same message: "You are looking for Jesus of Nazareth, who was crucified. He has been raised; he is not here" (16:6). What will we do with that news? Will we keep it a secret, out of fear of the implications? Or will we go tell it on the mountains?

Questions for Reflection and Discussion

1. Name three stories that are important for you to tell: about yourself, your family or other groups with whom you identify. How do these stories shape your sense of identity?

2. What kind of stories do you think our culture is too fond of telling? Which stories ought to be told more often? Give one example of each.

3. Saint Paul preached the importance of Jesus rather than reviewing his life and teachings. What's more important to you: what Jesus did and said, or who he is and what he means to us today? Explain your answer.

4. Mark wrote his Gospel in part to reveal the secret of who Jesus is. Flip through the Gospel of Mark and find a story that best uncovers the nature of Jesus for you.

5. Describe one way you do your part to tell the story of who Jesus was and is. Has there ever been a time when fear kept you from speaking what you know and have seen in faith?

Faith Response

Consider the ways in which you have been touched and healed spiritually, emotionally or physically; have been blind but now see; have had your "demons" (addictions, bad habits or attitudes) cast out. These are ways you have been called to witness to the power of Christ manifested in your life. Choose to be less afraid to say what you know to others.

The Argument Continues

Music appreciation is something many people come by naturally. Some folks, however, need help in getting a handle on how to listen to music. Before I enrolled in a music appreciation course, melody without words seemed pointless to me. The sound was just a jumble of high notes and low notes with no particular meaning. I could not enjoy what I was hearing, because I could not distinguish one thing from another. The colors and tones and messages delivered by the instruments did not communicate their gift to me. I felt outside the experience other people were having.

For some people, listening to the Gospels can create the same "outsider" feeling: "It's just the same story four times over, right?" But with just a little coaching, the different voices and messages of the Evangelists become clear and surrender their meaning. As with music, you have to know what to listen for.

In these next few chapters, we look at ways in which the gospel writers distinguished their message and why. Each wrote to a different audience with its own special needs and problems. Each addressed issues specific to his community through the story of Jesus. By examining the Gospels carefully, we come to appreciate how Jesus is Lord and teacher for each new generation, facing the contemporary situation head on. If we learn only one thing from the gospel writers, it's that Jesus continues to live in our generation of the Church, seeking to guide us on the road to greater and fuller life—just as he did with his followers two thousand years ago.

Origins of Matthew

From early on, Matthew had primacy over the other Gospels. For centuries, the church fathers quoted him more than any other source. Part of the reason Matthew enjoyed such favor, as we noted, is that his was the only Gospel at that time believed to be written by an Apostle and eyewitness to the ministry of Jesus. Matthew's Gospel is generally dated after the year 70, since the writer used Mark's Gospel as a source. Most scholars assign the Gospel to the decade of the 80s, because the level of anger against religious authorities in Matthew is far hotter than in Mark. (The early Christians were angry with the leaders of the Temple and synagogue for many reasons, which we will look at later in this chapter.)

In other respects, however, Matthew expresses views orthodox enough to have been written by a rabbi! Count how many times the Gospel says, "All of this took place to fulfill what was written," followed by a quote from Hebrew Scripture. Five such references surround the birth of Jesus alone. In Matthew, Jesus is presented as a teacher supportive of Jewish tradition and law: Jesus insists he has not come to abolish the law and even declares that those who keep the law faithfully will be the greatest in the kingdom.

Given the conflicting sides of the message, it is fair to ask: Who authored Matthew? The idea that Matthew the Apostle produced the Gospel is at best confusing. The late date argues against it, for one. And the text of Matthew borrows eighty percent of Mark's work, which leads us to wonder why an eyewitness would borrow from a second-generation Christian instead of relying on his own recollections. There is an outside source from around 125 that claims the Apostle Matthew wrote down the sayings of Jesus in Aramaic—a document yet to be discovered. The Gospel we call Matthew, written in Greek, may be derived in part from that earlier tradition, but the Apostle clearly did not write this gospel directly.

Expanded Horizons

Just flipping through Matthew alerts us to the idea that he's telling a bigger story than Mark tells. Mark begins his narrative with the ministry of Jesus; Matthew starts with a genealogy that places Jesus in the context of Jewish history. Matthew shows Jesus to be an essential part of the plan of salvation revealed to

Israel: There are fourteen generations between Abraham and David, fourteen more to the Babylonian Exile, and a final fourteen to the birth of Jesus. This neat parallelism demonstrates that Jesus was destined to be as integral to the Hebrew story as these other figures and events. Already we see the "rabbi" side of Matthew at work, promoting Jesus as the anticipated Jewish Messiah.

Next Matthew tells the Christmas story, which follows a literary form known as an "infancy narrative." (Other infancy narratives in the Bible surround characters like Samuel and Moses, inviting us to pay attention—this person is going to be significant.) Matthew's infancy story is told mostly from the vantage point of Joseph, who is the main actor. An angel appears to Joseph three times in dreams: bidding him to accept the expectant Mary into his home, warning him to flee to Egypt, and later inviting him to return. The Holy Family imitates the greater story of the Exodus in their journey, as the Israelites once went down to Egypt to escape famine and later returned to their land by the hand of God.

But Matthew not only retells the history of Israel symbolically through this narrative; he also foreshadows the gospel story to come. In the tale of the magi, for example, Matthew relates how the king of Israel seeks the death of Jesus, while foreign kings come to adore him. This account anticipates what happens later, when the leaders of Israel reject Jesus and call for his death, while Gentiles eagerly receive the revelation of the Christ. In two short chapters, Matthew manages to remind us of the Hebrew Scripture of old and to foretell the Christian story that is to come. He sets a wide stage for the expanding story of salvation.

Matthew continues to expand the borders of Mark's account throughout his Gospel. He takes Mark's mere mention that Jesus was tempted in the desert (see Mark 1:12–13) and turns it into a miracle play in his own chapter 4. The church fathers point out that Matthew pictured Jesus being tempted in the same ways Israel was challenged by sin in the desert wanderings of Exodus. Unlike Israel, however, Jesus emerges victorious from all three temptations.

Matthew also has a more expansive finish to his Gospel. He adds many details to the passion story and includes two post-resurrection appearances by Jesus. In the last one, Jesus gives his still-wavering disciples the instruction now known as the Great Commission: to go and make disciples of all nations. Mark's Gospel leaves us with an unfinished sensation, inviting our personal response to the empty tomb. But in Matthew, the last word clearly belongs to Jesus.

Matthew the Editor

There are advantages to not being first, especially as a writer. T.S. Eliot once said, "Good poets borrow. Great poets steal." We can credit this unusual spirit of generosity to writer's license, for certainly Matthew had Mark to "borrow" from extensively. He also had the Q source that Luke would share. But Matthew obviously had a third source for nearly half of his Gospel, a source scholars call "M": that aspect of the story unique to Matthew. Maybe M was the oral tradition handed down by the community once gathered around the Apostle Matthew. Maybe M was the writer's own inspired revelation. Maybe M represented a whole lot of research.

But Matthew also employed a resource every writer has—his or her present context. Every generation provides its own perspective—a set of values, allegiances and shared history distinctly meaningful to it. Even when telling a story that's been told countless times, each new generation will unconsciously edit it—sorting, adapting, adding or subtracting from the story to make it relevant to the present audience. Only a really bad storyteller goes on and on about details that have no reference points for those who are listening. In that regard, Matthew was a remarkably good storyteller. He made the case for Jesus with his own listeners and their situation very much in mind. If he had to make some changes in Mark's way of telling the story for the sake of his community, he wasn't skittish about doing so.

One way Matthew edits Mark is that he "rehabilitates" the disciples. In Mark's Gospel, the disciples seem at a loss to understand things—no matter what Jesus says or does. Their ignorance is almost stylized, like slapstick comedy. You know they are going to slip on the theological banana peel as soon as it appears in view. Perhaps Mark had intended his audience to reflect on how we are all ignorant when we first come to the Gospel. He may have been reminding us of the need for humility in our discipleship. And since Mark was probably writing in mission territory outside of Israel, he didn't mind if the Apostles came off as just a little ridiculous in his story.

But this characterization seems to bother our very Jewish Matthew. So he sets out to redeem the disciples in places where Mark lets them sink. For example, Mark recounts how James and John audaciously approach Jesus asking for the two best seats in his coming reign. But Matthew transfers the request to the lips of their *mother*—a convenient shifting of the blame. Matthew also represents Jesus as having great confidence in the Apostles: for example, only in Matthew's Gospel does Jesus call Peter "rock" and bestow on him the leadership of the community.

But Matthew doesn't stop at redeeming the character of the disciples; he edits Mark to "redeem" Jesus as well. Mark, you may notice, allows Jesus more humanity. Remember the wisecrack about Jesus' paternity that slips into the Nazareth rejection story in Mark 6:3 ("son of Mary")? Matthew amends it. The crowd now asks, "Is not this *the carpenter's son?* Is not his mother called Mary…?" (Matthew 13:55, emphasis added) Also, in Mark, Jesus is shown to be surprised at certain events, whereas Matthew displays a more all-knowing Lord. Compare the two stories about the hemorrhaging woman who secretly grasps Jesus by the cloak to be healed. In Mark's account, Jesus turns and asks, "Who touched my clothes?" (Mark 5:30) In Matthew's version, Jesus doesn't ask; he *knows*, and he commends the woman for her faith (see 9:22).

But Matthew's Gospel is not just a new edition of Mark's. Matthew has his own pressing agenda that requires a new approach to the gospel story.

Motivation for a New Gospel

Nobody asks why Mark wrote his Gospel; in the absence of a written record, Mark supplied what was missing. But it's natural to ask why the *next* Gospel was written, and the ones after that. After all, nobody asks why Herman Melville wrote *Moby Dick* in 1851. But if somebody *else* sat down and wrote another version of *Moby Dick,* as Sena Jeter Naslund did when she wrote *Ahab's Wife* in 1999, we have to ask "Why?" Obviously, Naslund had something new she wanted to tell us that could not be told from the old point of view. Behind every story, we ought to remember, is the author's purpose in telling it. So we have to presume that Matthew, in his Gospel, wanted to say something Mark didn't or couldn't have said.

Theories abound regarding Matthew's purpose. Since he had Mark's text in front of him, we can suppose that he found it insufficient for his community—or he wouldn't have bothered to write another. So something new had emerged in the situation of the early Church since the time of Mark's writing, something that urgently needed to be addressed. That event, scholars suspect, was the destruction of the Jerusalem Temple in 70 A.D.

Why was this event so shattering for Christians? For one thing, the first generation of the Church was composed largely of devout Jews. Matthew's Gospel, so full of asides about Jewish tradition and quotes from Hebrew Scripture, was certainly intended for a community of Jewish followers of Jesus whose relationship to the Temple was as reverent as any believer in Israel. The Jerusalem Temple was essential to Israel's covenant with God. It was the place where heaven and earth met and did business. The sacrifices at the Temple atoned for sin and kept the community reconciled with God.

Like any city, Jerusalem had seen its share of riots. Caiaphas had feared one would break out when Jesus came to town on the day we commemorate as Palm Sunday. In 70, historians tell us, the citizens did riot, possibly in response to a pagan sacrilege committed by the occupation forces, and the Romans reacted by destroying the Temple. Two immediate results ensued. One was that the identity of Israel before God was transformed. How would they now mediate between heaven and earth? The other result was that the followers of Jesus, blamed in part for the community's unrest, were forced to flee Judea altogether, taking up residence on the far side of the Jordan.

For the Jewish community, the cultic religion led by the Sadducees was finished. Without the Temple, there could be no sacrifice, no functioning priesthood. The Pharisees, who emphasized prayer and law over temple sacrifice, emerged as the unexpected leaders of the new Judaism. These rabbis reassembled at Jamnia in northern Judea to establish the new face of orthodoxy for the faithful, and these newly powerful leaders came down hard on the Jewish followers of Jesus. In fact, around the year 80, the rabbis at Jamnia instituted a ban effectively excommunicating followers of Jesus from the life of the synagogue. Before the ban, you could be a Jew and a disciple of Jesus; after the ban, you had to choose. What followed was a searing rebuke of rabbinical authority by those Christian believers who understood the revelation of Jesus Christ as an utterly Jewish matter. Matthew's Gospel, or at least the final revision of it, reflects that protest.

Matthew's Gospel, then, is a reply from the newly orphaned Christianity, unexpectedly cut off from its Jewish roots the way Judaism was cut off from its Temple tradition. The Pharisees face a diatribe of reverse rejection in this Gospel, being called "brood of vipers," "hypocrites," "blind guides," "white-washed tombs" and "serpents." Jesus marvels when he encounters the centurion seeking healing for his servant: "Truly I tell you, in no one in Israel have I found such faith" (8:10). He later warns his disciples that they will be flogged in the synagogues. In Matthew, the Pharisees alone get the blame for starting the campaign to kill Jesus—not the temple officials, as we read in other Gospels.

Matthew's chapter 23 contains some of the hardest language in the New Testament against the Jewish authorities, followed by a critical reworking of Mark's account of the passion. Only Matthew shows Pilate the Roman washing his hands of responsibility for Jesus' murder, while the Jewish crowds accept the guilt for themselves and their children. Joseph of Arimathea, a hero among early Christians for having the courage to bury Jesus, gets a makeover between the two Gospels. Mark presents Joseph unabashedly as "a respected member of the council" of the Sanhedrin. Matthew, however, finds this unacceptable and reintroduces Joseph as simply "a rich man from Arimathea" and a disciple of Jesus (see Mark 15:43; Matthew 27:57). In Matthew's account, when Jesus dies, the veil of the Temple is torn in two, prefiguring destruction and disgrace. He also includes one final indignity: In the end, the chief priests bribe the soldiers at the empty tomb to claim that the body of Jesus was stolen by his disciples. Matthew adds: "And this story is still told among the Jews to this day" (28:15).

It must have been bitter for the early disciples of Jesus to be shut out of the Jewish assembly, but we have to see it from both sides. As far as the rabbis were concerned, followers of Jesus were heretics to the faith of their fathers. So they passed a requirement that every faithful Jew pray daily for the shattering of the "kingdom of arrogance" represented by the Christian "heretics." It is sad when people of faith fall into such hostile opposition in their devotion to the same God, but that's as true today as it was two thousand years ago.

A Handbook for the Church

Content and tone are two ways in which Matthew's Gospel can be distinguished from Mark's, but a third way is style. Some scholars view Matthew as an early church lectionary, organized for use in public worship just like the book of readings we use at Mass. Others suspect this Gospel was intended as a handbook for church leaders. (Matthew is the only Gospel to employ the word "church" at all, which it does three times.) Whatever its original purpose, the book is divided into five main sections, each one a narrative of action followed by a "discourse," or teaching, by Jesus. The five discourses are identified as the Sermon on the Mount (see chapters 5–7); the teaching on mission (see chapter 10); the parables of the kingdom (see chapter 13); instruction on the community of the Church (see chapter 18); and the discourse on the end of the world and Judgment (see chapter 23–25). The discourses are an excellent handbook for those seeking to grasp the self-understanding of the Church in any age.

The teachings of Jesus take up a prominent portion of Matthew's Gospel. Compare that with Mark, who tells us Jesus taught in every town—but rarely does he tell us what Jesus said. For Matthew, Jesus' teaching authority distinguished him in the eyes of the crowds, and *what* he taught added to their astonishment. Jesus spoke passionately about the reign or kingdom of God that serves as a "moment of truth" for every human heart. The kingdom is mentioned in Matthew almost fifty times; the largest number of parables is given over to describing it. The kingdom is presented as a paradoxical revelation in which the last are first, the least are greatest, children are important instead of uncounted, and the poor have reason to rejoice. The kingdom doesn't square with common sense or worldly experience. Yet it is presented as God's ultimate vision for the world.

The Sermon on the Mount highlights this teaching in the Beatitudes, arguably Matthew's masterpiece. In it, the present circumstances of woe and hardship for the believing community would be turned into an endless season of blessing in the kingdom.

Jesus' teaching was important as a model for church leaders learning to wield their authority within the community. Jesus demonstrates how genuine authority bends low for the poor while challenging the powerful. The rants against Pharisees are pointed warnings to Church leaders as well not to get too comfortable in seats of privilege in the assembly, nor too fond of titles and marks of respect.

The Legacy

In the 1960s, filmmaker and avowed communist Pier Paulo Pasolini was once detained from taking his train in Italy. The pope was passing by and all bets were off when regular travel would resume. Disgruntled, Pasolini returned to his hotel room and picked up the only thing to read: a Bible. Turning to Matthew, he read with astonishment the vision of the Evangelist. It sounded like a call for social transformation dear to the heart of any revolutionary. The film that emerged from this chance encounter, *The Gospel According to Saint Matthew,* ironically made Pope John Paul II's list of forty-five best movies of the century. So the communist and the famous defender against communism join hands across a generation and agree on one thing: the moving power of Matthew's vision. It's nice to think that Matthew could be a force for reconciliation just as surely as he testified to division in his own time.

The writer of Matthew was born into an era when argument was the atmosphere of the Church. If he is fierce in his vision, he is also eloquent in his hope for the coming reign of God. His innovation of the Christmas story is a perfect antidote to the bitter times he inherited. Although the curtain of the Temple is in tatters, a star rises over Israel, revealing the king who will become the very presence of God-among-us, Emmanuel. Matthew may have been bred in conflicted times, but his story retains its hold on wonder. And if we can retain wonder in the face of our conflicted times, Matthew's legacy will be secure.

Questions for Reflection and Discussion

1. Which points in this chapter are most useful for you in coming to understand Matthew's Gospel and the plurality of the four Gospels?

2. The separation of Christianity from Judaism led to centuries of suffering and mistrust. How might both faith traditions today reconcile their past to create a better future?

3. Which teaching in Matthew speaks most powerfully to your own experience? Which teaching seems most important for church leaders today?

4. Read the parables of the kingdom in Matthew 13. Which parable helps you to best understand the kingdom as Jesus invites us to consider it? Explain your answer.

5. Conflicts arose throughout church history (the Great Schism of the Orthodox Church, the Protestant Reformation, mistrust arising from Vatican II). What conflicts exist within the Christian community today and what can be done about them?

Faith Response

Write "Beatitudes" for our generation based on those found in the Sermon on the Mount (see Matthew 5:3–12). Who gets the blessings, and what do the blessings entail? Meditate on what it means that today's poor are guaranteed the kingdom.

Way Beyond Jerusalem

"The journey is the destination." This phrase appears in hikers' guides and on tee shirts designed with the dedicated wanderer in mind. If you've ever been tempted to hike the length of the Appalachian Trail or to take the Bright Angel route across the Grand Canyon, you understand the sentiment. Even if a walk through Central Park or around the block is more your speed, the idea that we learn as we go is still accessible. Sometimes what we see along the way is better than the place we are heading. Orienting ourselves toward a goal can be more significant than achieving it.

The language of journey is "pilgrim talk." For two thousand years, people who set their sights on the Holy Land or a famous shrine traveled there in the spirit of *pilgrimage*, a journey of repentance, renewal and commitment. The word also has come to suggest our allotted time on earth. No matter how tightly we cling to the life we know, the reality is we're all just passing through. Where are we going, and where do we wind up after this? What is the point of all this labor and learning, these years and relationships? Some folks seem to make it through the day for the sole purpose of watching television or getting to the cocktail hour. Is there more to life than this?

Pilgrims know that the journey and the destination are inseparable. They also know that a pilgrimage is not something they take on alone, but with a community that shares the road with them—with all of its adversity and serendipity. There is no merit in arriving first or fast, because getting there isn't as important as going there. Whatever hardship they face or miracles they encounter on the way, pilgrims know that the lessons of the journey are part of the reason they are on this road to begin with.

Luke's writing is all about journey, and his purpose is to describe the road, the community, the price of admission, and the beauty of the way. Luke maps for us a demanding pilgrimage—one not for the soft and comfortable—that leads into the very heart of this world, not to mention the next.

A New Starting Point

The Gospel of Luke was written in the same decade as the Gospel of Matthew, probably between 80 and 85. It's a coin toss as to which came first, although Luke does mention in his opening remarks that "many have undertaken to set down an orderly account of the events" (1:1)—an indication that other gospels were around. There is no evidence, however, that Matthew or Luke employed each other as a source. Obviously Luke, like Matthew, was not satisfied with the gospels in circulation and felt there was more to say. Certainly Luke's context is distinctive. He is a Gentile Christian writing to a community of believers outside of Israel, most likely a mixed society of Jewish and Gentile faithful. Matthew writes in the midst of division; Luke seeks to be a reconciler for the two factions within his audience. And while Matthew widens the focus of Mark to include Jewish history starting with Abraham, Luke does him one better. He traces Jesus back to Adam, the original "son of God" (3:38). In this way, Jesus is revealed to be not simply the Messiah of the Jews, but the Savior of the world. "Prophet" and "Savior" become two significant titles for Jesus in Luke's Gospel, conveying his link to both Hebrew prophetic tradition and the universal need for hope.

Who was Luke? If you ask five scholars about authorship of a particular book of the Bible, you will usually get five different answers. But at least some scholars accept Luke to be who Scripture and tradition say he is: a physician and companion of Paul's. Heavyweight church fathers like Tertullian, Origin and Jerome confirm this opinion. Contemporary scholars, however, are more reluctant to confirm this assignment; for experts, the fun is in the debate.

Luke's affiliation with Paul should not make us leap to the conclusion that this is, in any way, "the gospel according to Paul." First of all, Paul was not an eyewitness to the ministry of Jesus, so his account would be second-hand at best. Second,

Luke's association with Paul may have been brief. Certainly there is no evidence in Luke's writing to suggest a great familiarity with Paul's understanding of Jesus. And from Paul's letters, we know Paul is much more interested in *Christology*—the meaning of God's Anointed One showing up in human history—than he is in the biography of Jesus.

Luke does make use of at least sixty percent of Mark's work and shares that elusive Q source with Matthew. But more than half of Luke comes from "L," the name scholars give to Luke's own special material. Although some have tried to ascribe the L source to conversations Luke had with Paul or Jesus' mother Mary, or some other gospel insider, those links have not been established.

What we do know is that Luke is concerned with demonstrating how the birth of Jesus had implications for the whole world. He tells us who the emperor of Rome and the governor of the province were, situating Jesus in his times like no other gospel does. He mentions contemporary events like the martyrdom of Jews in Galilee by Pontius Pilate and a tower collapsing in Siloam, crushing eighteen people. For Luke's community, it appears significant that Jesus landed not merely in the center of Jewish salvation history but smack in the middle of human history altogether.

Parallel Stories

When we think "Christmas," we think "Luke." Even Charlie Brown gets an earful of Luke when his younger brother Linus seeks to answer his question, "Does anybody know what Christmas is all about?" It's about madonnas and manger scenes and angels and shepherds and swaddling clothes. The view of Christmas that holds our imaginations most keenly is evidence of Luke's highly effective storytelling.

But Luke does not begin his Gospel with the infancy narrative of Jesus. Rather, he starts with the infancy narrative of John the Baptist, and tells the two stories back to back. This is an early example of a favorite device in Luke: the creation of parallel stories to compare and contrast.

For example, in the foretelling of John's birth, the angel

announces the news to Zechariah because infancy narratives generally highlight the father (see the role of Joseph in Matthew). But in Jesus' birth story, Mary is the recipient of the angel's message as well as the main actor in the event. This reversal of custom is underscored by the results of each manifestation: Zechariah questions the angel and is struck dumb until the child's birth for entertaining doubt; Mary asks basically the same question and is favored with a reply. The visit between the mothers, Mary and Elizabeth, confirms the truth of both angelic appearances. Thus, in a rare departure from Jewish tradition, the men of salvation history are effectively sidelined in favor of the women.

Another parallel is drawn between the holy man Simeon and the prophetess Anna in the Temple at the time of Jesus' presentation. The pattern is already established: first, the story of a man, followed by one about a woman in a similar circumstance. Luke also presents paired healing stories (see chapter 7) and sets of parables (see chapter 18). We even see parallels in discipleship. Not long after Jesus chooses the Twelve, Luke tells us that many women also followed Jesus and supported his ministry out of their own pockets. If Jesus has a favored relationship with Peter, James and John in most Gospels, it is matched by his affection for the sisters Martha and Mary in Luke. Luke is telling a story of inclusion, and his first radical inclusion is the presence and significance of the women around Jesus.

A New Israel

Not having to defend Christianity in the face of closed doors as Matthew did, Luke is free to spend his energy opening some doors of his own. Naturally, Luke didn't "invent" the Gentile mission of Jesus, but he gives it top priority in his gospel of inclusion. Are you unclean, a Samaritan, a woman, a Gentile, a tax collector, a sinner, or some other undesirable? Jesus is here to eat with you, cure you, or accept you into his most intimate circle. In Luke, Jesus tells parables with Samaritan heroes, a repulsive idea to his audience. Jesus is revealed as an equal-opportunity Messiah.

Luke's intention should not be misunderstood, however. He is not suggesting that Israel is no longer the chosen people of God. Nor is he saying that the distinction between Israel and the outside world is no longer significant. For a Gentile writer, Luke shows a remarkable respect for all things Jewish. Rather than negate Israel, he broadens the meaning of Israel itself. Scholars say he *reconstituted* Israel, so that the true sons and daughters of Abraham are now understood to be all who wholeheartedly await the kingdom of God. For Luke, we could say, Israel is no longer a country but a state of mind. If you embrace the salvation of the world emerging from Israel, your faith is a passport into the *new* Israel.

It is a new Israel in more ways than one. Through Luke's spiritualized vision, not only ethnicity but also time and geography are redefined. Luke is sometimes characterized as a gifted writer who was nonetheless a sloppy historian with a poor sense of geography. For example, he names the wrong governor for the time period he describes, and he shows Jesus taking random journeys through ambiguous towns and crossing borders haphazardly. Others have suggested that Luke worked always with an eye to "theological necessity" in telling his story, rather than slavish servitude to chronology and maps. So perhaps Luke employs a landscape with "theologically" selected routes and features, so that Jesus encounters Jews, Samaritans or Gentiles on cue to suit the narrative need for juxtaposition.

To be fair, it must be said that Matthew also uses "theologically appropriate" geography, as when he begins Jesus' teaching ministry on a mount, suggestive to a Jewish audience that Jesus teaches with the authority of Moses, who received God's law on a mountain. After the resurrection, Matthew places the appearance of Jesus on a mountain to reinforce the point. So when Luke moves Matthew's Sermon on the Mount to a plain ("a level place" in 6:17), he does not change the terrain of literal Israel, of course. But theologically he may be suggesting that all who come to Jesus—Jews and Gentiles, men and women, righteous and sinners—receive his teaching on a level playing field. Truth no longer comes down from heaven on stone tablets for the privileged few, as it did in Moses' time. It is no surprise or accident that Luke invites the people of Tyre and Sidon—Gentiles—to his Sermon on the Plain.

Conditions of the Journey

Some casual readers of Luke may find his Gospel the most comforting of the four. Matthew capitalizes on Jesus' teaching role, and maybe some of us have spent far too long in classrooms already. By comparison, Luke prefers to show Jesus as a healer and storyteller. The emphasis on inclusion, compassion and forgiveness in Luke's portrayal makes Jesus seem like a "kinder, gentler Lord." But make no mistake: Luke's Jesus is no pushover!

In the Gospel of Luke, Jesus speaks often of the terms of the journey, and what he describes is no spiritual walk in the park. Luke's Jesus wages war on the world of possessions. Where Matthew's Beatitudes read, "Blessed are the poor in spirit," Luke writes only, "Blessed are you who are poor" (Matthew 5:3; Luke 6:20.) Jesus may be criticized by his enemies for not fasting as a holy man should, but he instructs his disciples to keep a Spartan reserve: "Take nothing for your journey, no staff, nor bag, nor bread, nor money—not even an extra tunic" (9:3; see also 10:4). The bag prohibition seems plausible; but no sandwich, no sweater in case it gets chilly? These are tough terms for discipleship.

When some attempt to join Jesus on his journey, they come with their own conditions—a grave mistake in Lukan terms. Their requests sound reasonable: to fulfill their final duties to their parents, or to take leave of their families. But Jesus dismisses anyone who comes to him with a fist closed on a personal agenda. The journey he is on is too urgent to waste time even discussing personal exceptions.

Jesus speaks plainly in Luke: This journey involves the burden of the cross. If you are prepared to lose your life, you can save it. But if you are intent on saving your life, you are already lost. Finally, Jesus lowers the boom: "None of you can become my disciple if you do not give up all your possessions" (14:33). *All my possessions?* This Lord may be gentle and forgiving, but his terms are more than most of us can bear.

The Compassion of God

Is there a more compassionate face of God than the one Luke reveals? In this Gospel alone we hear how God forgives us huge debts of sin; is a friend in need even in the middle of the night; seeks us out like a lost coin; and shows mercy to the poor sinner more than to the self-righteous. Jesus showcases the compassion of the good Samaritan who cares about the suffering man in the ditch—even though he happens to be a Jew and therefore his enemy.

But of all the parables Jesus tells about the wild and liberating mercy of God, the one that drove his audience to distraction—then as now—is the story of the prodigal son. We know the story by heart: a son receives his inheritance early and squanders it on things that are an abomination to his family. Then, bankrupt, he has the gall to show up at his father's door and ask for work. What just kills us and offends our legalistic sense of justice is that the father spots his son from a distance and resolves to forgive him utterly. Abandoning dignity, he runs outside and throws his arms around the grimy young man, not even listening to his prepared speech. As a final assault on our sense of just deserts, the father throws this useless son a party. No wonder the man's other son is beside himself!

But Jesus doesn't just talk mercy. He lives it. At the Last Supper, Jesus tells Peter that he has prayed for him, knowing Peter will deny him. There is a tender moment, recorded in no other Gospel, when Jesus meets Peter's eyes after the denial. In Matthew and Mark, all we hear from the lips of Jesus on the cross is the attested cry from Psalm 22: "My God, my God, why have you abandoned me?" Whereas in Luke, Jesus speaks three times from the cross, twice in forgiveness (first for his murderers, second on behalf of the good thief), and a third time in perfect surrender of his spirit (from Psalm 31). God's mercy is our destination, Luke suggests, and it also must be our path.

Beyond the Cross

After Jesus is arrested, the Twelve scatter. We are not surprised, however, when Luke informs us that the women who have been with Jesus since Galilee remain until his death—parallelism to the end. Luke alone mentions three women by name who return to the tomb on Easter morning, and he recounts two significant post-resurrection appearances: to the couple traveling to Emmaus (still journeying but needing a push in the right direction), and to the disciples back in Jerusalem. Luke includes in his account our only gospel ascension story.

But Luke's post-resurrection story goes much further. The Acts of the Apostles is a second New Testament book attributed to Luke, and we can think of it as "Luke: The Sequel." His first book takes us on the journey of Jesus to Jerusalem and his destiny. The second journey in Acts will follow the mission of the disciples all the way to Rome, the center of the ancient world. This inclusive gospel cannot remain within the boundaries of Israel, but must spread to the whole world so that all will know Jesus as Savior.

By the time of Luke's writing, the Church was getting used to the idea that Jesus might not be coming back right away. Luke's presentation of discipleship as journey prepares the Church for the long road that may lie ahead. If every journey is a participation in the arrival we are seeking, then the kingdom is in our midst—not just "at hand" but "within" us—even as we anticipate its coming. "The Arrival from ahead of us," as theologian Jurgen Moltmann named the kingdom, is most certainly on its way all the time. But in a real way, for those with eyes to see, we are already standing at the heart of it.

Questions for Reflection and Discussion

1. Consider a planned or unplanned journey you have taken. What did you learn while on the way there? How did the journey affect your arrival?

2. Luke saw Jesus as central to human history and significant for the whole world. How does this affect the mission of the Church and your own mission as a believer?

3. The gospel of inclusion makes room for undesirable people of the first century. Name the sort of people who would be included if Luke were writing in our century.

4. How easy or difficult would it be for you to follow Jesus under Luke's terms and conditions? Do you think Jesus is too demanding or too lenient in this Gospel? Explain your answer.

5. How would you describe your journey of faith so far? Use the idea of "theological geography" to create a road map of where your life has taken you and where it seems headed.

Faith Response

Make a commitment to include those who are normally left out in your family, your community, your parish or the greater society. Consider concrete ways your mealtime can become "another eucharist"—an avenue of invitation for those who are not often welcomed.

The Cosmic Christ

"Does anybody really know what time it is? Does anybody really care...about time?" So goes the lyric to a classic song by the band Chicago. The answer, these days, is yes; most of us do care very much about time. We awaken to alarm clocks and strap on wristwatches. We glance up to check the clock in every private room or public square. Our computers and stoves and VCRs insist on telling us the time, as if we might somehow forget it.

Yet we are hardly in danger of forgetting about time. Our routines are circumscribed by an awareness of time, from the moment we wake up to our last glance at the clock that reminds us we ought to be in bed by now. Our days depend on appointments and hours of availability—when the train leaves, how long practice runs after school, and what time the movie starts. Imagine trying to get through one modern day without access to a clock.

But there's more to time than the minutes of the day. A friend moans because she's another year older. We pause to acknowledge the anniversaries of marriages or deaths. When we take ill, there is always the possibility that this is it, that we are permanently running out of time. And no matter what we do with our time, we can't get any of it back.

Time is crucial. It flies. It drags. It offers endless potential and then gradually takes it all away. But as the Hail Mary prayer reminds us, there are really only two significant moments in time: *now* and *at the hour of our death.* One moment is the time for action, and the other is a time for which we need preparation. Some day, we know, those two moments that seem so far removed from each other will be one and the same. The time to consider the consequences of that merging, however, is *now*, and not then.

If the Gospel of John has a theme, it is that Jesus is keenly aware, from the moment he begins his ministry, where all of his

39

effort is headed. He speaks frequently of his "hour," which is the time of his fulfillment. It is also, eerily, the time of his death. For Jesus knows that the cross is the only door through which his glory awaits. The time will be right, paradoxically, when it is over. Or, as he says in his final words from the cross, his words ripe with meaning: "It is finished" (John 19:30).

An Insider's Gospel

If the first three Gospels are called Synoptic because they are alike, then it's obvious who's different. John's Gospel is so radically different that it caused controversy before it was admitted into the canon of Scripture. John's testimony is a great departure from the three that precede it. What's worse, it is similar in character to second-century texts popular among the *Gnostics* (a movement named from the Greek word for knowledge.) The Gnostics took Christianity and turned it into a kind of mystery religion popular at the time, complete with a dualistic view of the world (light vs. darkness, good vs. evil engaged in cosmic struggle), the need for special knowledge to be liberated from what we might call today "the dark side," the rejection of material reality, and a tendency to borrow ideas and practices from other traditions (a practice called *syncretism*). What most made the Gnostics heretical to orthodox Christianity is that they utterly rejected the humanity of Jesus, preferring to think of his appearance in history as a sort of divine mirage meant for our instruction.

Still, John's Gospel was admitted to the Christian canon nonetheless. It had a few things in its favor: an early enough production date (scholars presume 90 to 100, which makes it the last canonical Gospel to be written), and the backing of Irenaeus, a second-century bishop notoriously opposed to the Gnostics. (If the Gospel of John was good enough for Irenaeus, the thinking went, then surely it passed the test of orthodoxy.) It also profited from an early bit of author confusion. The gospel writer was mistakenly identified with the Apostle John— Zebedee's son and James' brother. Scholars now believe the community contributing to the formation of this Gospel was led by a charismatic figure from Ephesus also named John. It seems clear from the various existing versions of this manuscript that the Gospel was a collaborative effort, or at least underwent several significant revisions. The prologue and chapter 21 were added later, and the story of the woman taken in adultery almost certainly did not belong to this Gospel at all. (Some speculate that it fits better in Luke and have "reassigned" it there.)

Unlike the other Gospels that were written for the dual purposes of instruction (for the faithful) and evangelization (for winning converts), John has the ring of a pure insider's gospel. It presupposes prior knowledge of the story of Jesus, and it speaks disdainfully of the outside world, something you might not want to do when in dialogue with it. But the real purpose of the text may have been to persuade its own community that Jesus was not only sent by God but *is* God, incarnate and unmistakable. Up to then, the other Gospels had used the term "Son of God" without being too precise about what that means. John makes the identification crystalline, redefining the meaning of monotheism (the Jewish principle that God is one) forever.

Epic Proportions

By way of recap: Mark begins the story of Jesus at the time of his ministry. Matthew inserts Jesus deeper into Hebrew history by tracing Joseph's genealogy back to Abraham. Luke pulls his lens further back and reveals Jesus squarely in human history, tracing his lineage to Adam and situating him within the Roman Empire. John outdoes them all, panning his perspective all the way back to *prehistory*. He begins his narrative in the time before time existed, when God was present with the divine Word as yet unspoken, and creation not yet called into being. Jesus, we are told, is this "Word." The Word of God is first uttered in the activity of creation, and then countless more times in the oracles of the prophets. Finally, John tells us, the Word entered the world and "pitched his tent among us"—the literal rendering of 1:14—taking on mortality and bringing us hope of eternity.

This was a radical development in Christology. The idea of

41

the preexistence of the Word of God submits that before there was a historical person named Jesus there was a Christ whom we affirm in faith. This "Christ of faith" includes everything Jesus was on earth but also everything he was and is in the realm of God before and since. Jesus is not only "Son of God" but also "one with God" in a way never so boldly expressed. The major theme of John's Gospel is to highlight this doctrine and so reveal Jesus "in glory."

What is glory, exactly? In human terms, it's a synonym for praise and a piece of the limelight. But God's glory isn't a product of the praise we lavish upon the deity in prayer. God's glory is described in the Hebrew Scriptures as fire or cloud surrounding and enshrouding the divine Presence, like the pillar of fire that guided the Israelites through the desert or the cloud that surrounded the Tent of the Presence in Moses' time (see Exodus 40:34-38). This brightness is an attribute of God's nature; it simultaneously conceals God from us (for if we looked at God, Scripture notes, we would surely die), and manifests God's holiness to us. This brightness is revealed in Jesus through the event known as the Transfiguration, which all three Synoptic Gospels report. In John's story, however, there is no Transfiguration, since Jesus is manifesting the glory of God all the while.

John's Gospel is composed of two sections known as the Book of Signs (see 1:19–12:50) and the Book of Glory (see 13:1–20:31). In the Book of Signs, Jesus performs seven carefully chosen miracles as evidence of his authority and identity. These seven signs—water changed into wine, the cure of the official's son, the healing of the cripple at Bethesda, the miracle of the loaves, walking on water, the restoration of the man born blind, and the raising of Lazarus—are offered to bring the disciples to faith in anticipation of the "hour" of glory, when Jesus will be "lifted up" (literally on the cross and ultimately to his rightful place in heaven). The Book of Glory defines and celebrates the meaning of that fateful hour.

If John's Gospel sounds headier and more mysterious than the others, then you are hearing it correctly. Of course, none of the Gospels—indeed, nothing in the Bible—is written as pure theology. Scripture is primarily *testimony* based on personal experience and not simply intellectual theory. But John's Gospel has often been thought of as an extended theological reflection on the significance of Jesus, rather than the story of his ministry and passion as in the other Gospels. In order to understand what John is doing, perhaps we should begin by observing what he does *not* do—according to the "gospel standard" outlined in the Synoptic tradition.

What's Missing in John

John is the book least mentioned when people name their favorite Gospel. Mark is preferred by students because of its brevity, its wonderfully clear narrative, and the beauty of its details. Just look at the tender descriptions of these three stories in Mark 5: the possessed man of Gerasene, who is shown as an object of pity, crying out and bruising himself with rocks; the long suffering of the woman with the hemorrhage and how doctors have treated and cheated her for years; the pathos in the story of Jairus's daughter who is, we are told, twelve years old—on the verge of womanhood but about to die, with so much potential for life yet to be lived. In response to such encounters, Jesus is alternately moved to pity, surprise, anger or sadness, revealing the depth of his humanity. Mark's attention to poignant, humanizing detail makes his Gospel easy to love.

Matthew is a favorite with those who appreciate sound moral instruction. His Sermon on the Mount in chapters 5-7 alone puts him in the biblical writer's Hall of Fame. The stories of Joseph's dreams, the star of Bethlehem, the gifts of the Magi, and the slaughter of the innocents (see chapters 1-2) are essential elements to the drama of *epiphany*, or God's movement among us in salvation history. The images we cherish about God's kingdom—the pearl of great price, the woman baking bread, the treasure hidden in the field, the shepherd searching for the lost sheep (see chapters 13 and 18-25 for the whole gamut of kingdom images)—are unique to Matthew's teaching stories. From him we also get the magnificent vision of Last Judgment (see 25:31-46) and the Great Commission of the Church's ministry in the world (see 28:16-20). It would be accurate to say that Matthew's story is "the gospel of the Church."

Social justice advocates and political progressives attach readily to Luke. His is the story of a Jesus who gets his hands dirty. Jesus promotes what we call today "the preferential option for the poor"—God's special embrace for the sick, the lowly, foreigners, and "the unclean," those on the outs in polite society. Luke lambastes the rich and powerful while affirming the compassion of God for the disadvantaged. At the same time, Luke holds the disciples of Jesus to the strictest possible standards and decries personal material gain. Luke is likewise a moving Gospel, the source of our most popular Christmas story as well as the primary biblical root of Marian devotion and spirituality. And where would the pilgrim Church be without Luke's Emmaus story (see 24:13-35), which shows how the Eucharist is the present-day revelation of Jesus among us.

Standing in this company, John's Gospel can seem downright forbidding. Heart-warming touches are noticeably absent, as are the humanizing details of Jesus' compassion for others and his own agony in the garden of Gethsemane. In John, Jesus tells no parables. He ceases to be a teacher for the masses altogether, preferring to spend his instruction on his inner circle. Nor does Jesus heal for the sake of revealing God's mercy. Rather, the healing stories in John's Gospel are "signs' intended to show the authority Jesus wields as the incarnation of God's powerful word.

Stories we consider part and parcel of the Gospel are missing from John: the baptism of Jesus by John, the transfiguration, the bread and wine of the Last Supper. But most significant of all, Jesus does not declare his mission to announce the kingdom of God. In John's eyes, Jesus comes to reveal *himself*. Jesus uses the key words I AM in speaking of himself, which the Jewish authorities correctly interpret as a reference to the name of God given to Moses: "I AM WHO AM" (Exodus 3:14). Either Jesus is an outrageous blasphemer, or he is the incarnation of God as he claims. The glory of God is hereby announced to those who can accept it.

Certainly, John has de-emphasized the humanity of Jesus in favor of heightening our awareness of his divinity. We recognize that the times are harder for John's audience, and the stakes are perhaps a little higher. Gone is the hope of a mission within Israel. Persecution—once rampant from sources within Judaism, like the rabbis at Jamnia—is now equally to be feared from the empire at large. Christian communities have become like secret societies, closed circles of faithful within a world hostile to their beliefs. In the Last Supper dialogues of John, Jesus assures his disciples that they do not belong to the world any more than he does. He is one with his Father, and they are one with him. The battle between the world and the spirit of holiness is engaged, and all must give allegiance to one or the other.

Clues to Interpreting John

Matthew and Luke wrote their Gospels to augment or nuance Mark's story. But there is no evidence that John's community intended their Gospel to replace other versions. Rather, readers of John were presumed to be familiar with the Jesus story from other sources. In fact, ninety percent of John's material is entirely new and offers fresh perspectives on the older stories. For example, consider the absence of an infancy narrative in John—at least, there is no explicit one. But scholars have interpreted the first miracle at Cana as a way of retelling the birth of Jesus through the eyes of faith. In it, we learn how Mary brings forth the ministry of Jesus with the interior sense of timing known to expectant mothers. Jesus does not choose the time; Mary does. And through her efforts, the first sign of Jesus' authority is revealed to the world as surely as any epiphany. In fact, the story of Cana was one of the original readings used for the Feast of the Epiphany by the churches of the East.

How are we to understand the strange omission of bread and wine at the Last Supper? John, the most eucharistic of the Gospels, substitutes the account of the meal with the washing of the disciples' feet. Of course, two of John's other stories—the wine at Cana and the multiplication of loaves and fish—are eucharistic in character, revealing the abundant life available through Jesus. John complements these stories with the Bread of Life discourse in chapter 6. There Jesus proclaims, as literally as in any Last Supper story, "I am the bread of life" (6:35). So when we come to the Last Supper, Jesus does not need to declare himself in the bread and wine again. Instead, he demonstrates what partaking in this meal must mean for its participants: the call to humble service.

One of the more disturbing features of John's Gospel is its orientation toward "the Jews." Because of John's presentation of the vehement response of "the Jews" against Jesus, especially in the passion account, this Gospel was later used to support anti-Semitism. Like so much material in John, however, "the Jews" are a symbol representing the religious leaders that called for Jesus' death. Positive portrayals of Jewish individuals—like Joseph of Arimathea and Nicodemus—within the story belie the blanket condemnation of "the Jews" (not to mention Jesus and his family and friends from Galilee themselves). Although this Gospel does not make use of frequent quotations of Hebrew Scripture and law, as the Synoptics do, John does use Hebrew history more implicitly, as when Jesus compares himself to the figures of Abraham, Moses and the prophets. Similarly, when John the Baptist declares, "Here is the Lamb of God!" (1:36), the symbol of Passover evokes the Exodus story of liberation. The bottom line is that—far from being hostile or indifferent to Hebrew tradition—John's Gospel presumes an intuitive grasp of it.

The Beloved Disciple and Us
Much has been made of a character John identifies only as "the beloved disciple." Historically, this person was presumed to be John the Apostle and the Gospel's author. Later, this disciple was identified with the charismatic leader whose community in Ephesus formed this Gospel in his honor, casting him in a starring role as "the one whom Jesus loved." But others have suggested that the beloved disciple is purposely left unidentified because he stands in for us, the readers of this story. As we come to the Gospel in faith, each of us has the opportunity to recline on Jesus' breast (like the disciple in 13:23) and know ourselves as his beloved. In this light, perhaps the Gospel of John is not so austere and unapproachable as it may seem. In the hour of his greatest glory, Jesus seeks to draw each of us very close.

Questions for Reflection and Discussion

1. Is time your adversary, your friend, or both? How does the reality of death shape your relationship to time?

2. On a scale of one to ten, how "Gnostic" are you? Check yourself against the central tenets of Gnostic heresy: dualistic view of the world, reliance on "special truth," rejection of the material realm, a tendency to syncretism. (For help, see the section on "An Insider's Gospel.")

3. Which of the seven signs in John's Gospel—water changed into wine, the cure of the official's son, the healing of the cripple at Bethesda, the miracle of the loaves, walking on water, the restoration of the man born blind, and the raising of Lazarus—are most significant in revealing who Jesus is in your life? Explain why you chose this sign.

4. Which of the four Gospels is the one you feel the most affinity toward? The least? Which elements of each are most instructive for you? Explain your answer.

5. Read John's resurrection narrative in chapter 20:1–10. Put yourself in the place of the beloved disciple and describe what you see at the tomb.

Faith Response

John's Gospel is full of signs that reveal Jesus as the glory of God present in the world. Where is this glory present today? Visit a place where you see "glory" clearly, and celebrate the vision with praise and a thankful heart.

The Hero Is the Word

Our world is in short supply of heroes. In an age that exalts celebrity and sometimes notoriety, the very notion of heroism is threatened. We are sold on *image* more than *substance*: folks with the right clothes, cool attitude, and large wallets. We are out of the habit of celebrating those who are genuinely remarkable: dedicated parents, selfless public servants, or good neighbors. It's as if we've forgotten that greatness is more about what one *does* than what one *has*.

In the ancient world, heroes weren't necessarily more plentiful, but they were held in higher public esteem. Books were written praising their deeds, and what these works lacked in historical precision they more than made up for in enthusiasm and exhortation. One such category of books recounted the deeds of heroes under the framework of their "acts." Like our New Testament book, the Acts of the Apostles, these works served to promote not only their heroes—people like Alexander and Hannibal—but also the emulation of their example and virtue.

What makes the Acts of the Apostles in the New Testament exceptional is that the real hero of the work is not any of its characters. Although Acts tells the story of many first-generation church heroes—giants of the faith like Peter, John, James, Stephen and Paul—the focus of the book is the journey the gospel takes from Jerusalem to Rome. The word of God had started out as a parochial matter for Jews to debate in their houses of prayer: Was Jesus, in fact, the Messiah of God? But before we reach the end of the Acts of the Apostles, God's word is being proclaimed at the heart of the Roman Empire and to the known world. How it got there is the subject of the book—and where it goes from there is for the reader to decide.

Acts in Context

Even the Bible has its literary critics. For example, some theologians grouse that Luke's decision to write the Acts of the Apostles was a bit of a sellout. Didn't he trust the core gospel message to be sufficient? Why go on about what happened next? Others view Acts with more respect, christening it "the gospel of the Holy Spirit." In style and theme, it is tightly related to Luke's "gospel of the Son," indicating that he envisioned the two books as a consolidated work. Luke did not intend his Gospel to be separated from Acts, as it is in our Bibles. But in the early second century, when the four canonical Gospels began circulating as a set, Acts was detached from Luke to make the collection more symmetrical.

Acts was written in the same time period as Luke, likely within the decade before 90 A.D. It describes events between the years 30 and 63 that were critical for the Church's self-understanding. Both Luke and Acts are self-consciously written for a specific patron, as their prologues reveal, unlike the rest of the New Testament, which began as internal church documents. But this does not make Luke's work more objectively "historical" as we understand that term. We have other documents paralleling the time frame of Acts that we can use as proof texts, especially Paul's letters, which cover a lot of the same territory. Paul is, after all, a primary source for the period, offering a rare (if unplanned) glimpse of biblical autobiography. Luke's material depends at least in part on secondary sources, even though he companioned Paul for a short time. Therefore, when discrepancies occur between Luke's and Paul's testimony—and there are significant ones—the jury of scholarship tends to side with Paul.

Did Luke shade the history of the early Church in order to reconcile bristling factions of his own community? If so, how? As in Luke's Gospel, Acts reflects a concern that both Jewish and Gentile Christians feel embraced by the message. As one scholar notes, Luke does his best to make Peter seem more Gentile in his leanings and Paul more Jewish in his dealings than either would have cared to have been presented. Does Luke want his message to seem more palatable to the Jewish community?

Undoubtedly. Does he engage in flattery of Roman figures in order to gain a hearing with his Gentile audience? No question. Is the purpose of Luke's two-volume set purely apologetics for either or both groups? That would be a harder case to make. Luke's frequent reiterations of Jewish salvation history and why Jesus fulfills it perfectly do indeed make the case for Jewish acceptance of the Gospel. And Luke's continual refrain that the activity of the Apostles is neither unlawful nor threatening to the civil order (put on the lips of virtually every Roman official in Acts) is a heavy-handed way of encouraging good citizens of the Roman Empire to give Christianity a look, no matter what they have heard about it. But for all that, Luke goes way beyond apologetics. His Acts of the Apostles is nothing short of a chronicle of the irresistible force that is passing through the known world like a cyclone: the mighty power of the Holy Spirit.

The Church Alight

Pentecost is the watershed event in Luke's two-volume *opus*. It occurs at the mid-point, in chapter 2 of Acts. But Luke has been preparing us for it from the start of his Gospel. Mary is informed she will conceive by the power of the Holy Spirit. John the Baptist proclaims that the one who is to come will baptize with the Holy Spirit and fire. After the resurrection, Jesus instructs his disciples not to leave the city "until you are clothed with power from on high" (Luke 24:49). Fifty days later, the amazing event that transforms common people into miracle workers occurs.

The first noticeable result of Pentecost is the gift of "tongues," the ability to speak to multitudes of every nation and be understood. We shouldn't be surprised that language is the first sign of the Holy Spirit's descent on the Church. The Church's mission is to preach the gospel far and wide. Since getting the word of God from Jerusalem to Rome (and from there, to the ends of the earth) is the Church's central task, undoing the curse of Babel (see Genesis 11) is critical.

But the Spirit brings far more to the Church than language. Extraordinary courage overwhelms the same group that once ran in fear of their lives. In short order, the Church has its first martyrs: Stephen, "filled with the Holy Spirit," is stoned some-time during the years 33-35; and James, brother of John and son of Zebedee, is put to death by Herod around the years 42-44.

Along with inspired speech and courage come signs and wonders. Miraculous healings occur where Peter's shadow falls. Philip casts out unclean spirits and outruns a chariot in the business of evangelization. When an Apostle goes to jail, an angel shows up to release him. Peter brings a beloved deceased member of the community back to life. When Paul preaches too long and a slumbering youth falls to his death out a win-dow, Paul restores him and returns him to his family.

The power of the Apostles is likewise eerie: when Ananias and Sapphira lie to the Church, Peter confronts them with the truth and they are struck dead. When a magician obstructs Paul's work, he is rendered blind for a time. It is important to remember, of course, that Paul himself was temporarily blinded to facilitate his conversion process. The Spirit works in mysteri-ous ways indeed.

Perhaps the most crucial activity of the Spirit is in the work of discernment. In Acts, the Spirit directs Peter's visit to Cor-nelius as well as the journey undertaken by Paul and Barnabas. The Spirit warns Paul of bad times to come as he nears Jerusalem. Even oracles come in a new formula: "Thus says the Holy Spirit…" (21:11). When the Apostles (including Paul) lay hands on baptized believers, the Spirit's gifts are released afresh in them.

The Spirit's empowerment of the mission to spread the faith must be kept in mind when dealing with the vaguely unsatisfying end of the Acts of the Apostles. Many, in fact, have wondered about a possible "lost ending" to Acts. It seems odd that the story closes before the fate of Paul, imprisoned in Rome and threatened with death, is resolved. If Luke is writing in 90, he knows the rest of the story. Yet, when we recall Luke's inten-tion—to deliver the word of God to the center of the known world by the power of the Holy Spirit—we see that the story's end is achieved. Paul is simply the messenger. Only the message merits our consideration.

Luke's Footprints

As a writer, Luke does not tread lightly. His themes recur throughout both his written works like relentless motifs. Read either book and highlight these portrayals: Jesus or the disciples at prayer; instances of joy and delight at the outcome of an event; the role of angels in promoting God's will; unusual inclusions of men and women or Jewish and Gentile figures; the celebration of meals and parties; travel as a mode of discipleship; and especially the guidance of the Holy Spirit. Luke underscores that the life of faith involves these fundamental elements.

Luke also presents themes that are subtler but no less deliberate. For example, Luke the reconciler wants his mixed assembly of Jewish and Gentile believers to get along. Luke also prefers harmony on the political level, and Paul's letters attest that the early church was far from a tranquil environment (see the next chapter for more about Paul's take on church politics). Luke chooses to gloss over the conflict in order to present the ideal of peace and order. Scholars suspect that the glitter of the "golden age" in the early Church may owe more to Luke's ideals than to the lived reality.

Read Acts with an eye to the frequent summaries of the Church's progress that appear at the end of many sections. There are references to the increase in numbers: "...that day about three thousand persons were added" (2:41); "...and day by day the Lord added to their number" (2:47); "...they numbered about five thousand" (4:4); "...a great many of the priests became obedient to the faith" (6:7). Luke presents the Church as ceaselessly flowering.

Luke also speaks of a communal life that the world has yet to capture in its regular attempts at creating a secular utopia. Luke writes that upon being baptized each member sold his or her property and laid it at the feet of the disciples. The early Church then held all goods in common and met regularly for prayer and eucharistic meals. Luke summarizes his thesis with the comprehensive statement: "The church throughout Judea, Galilee, and Samaria had peace and was built up" (9:31).

Perhaps modern cynicism makes us doubt that the early Church ever approached that level of perfection. But it is just as likely that the quality of religious fervor necessary to sell one's goods and live in utter abandonment to the Holy Spirit is something generally limited to the few.

Conflict Management

Evidence of conflict is widespread in the New Testament. The haves and the have-nots are historically in tension, and when two powers face off—even in the Church—one must bow before the other or be challenged.

The first sign of that tension shows up in the stories about John the Baptist and Jesus. We who have canonized John as a saint and call Jesus our Savior may not see the problem at first. John was the voice in the wilderness announcing the coming of Jesus, right? So where's the conflict? Well, in the early Church things weren't quite this black and white. Both John and Jesus drew followers from the same region, and sometimes Jesus gained disciples from John (see John 1:35–37). It is apparent that the Baptist, despite his testimony to Jesus, did not abandon his own work of baptizing to become a disciple of Jesus himself. Rather, John remains an "inter-testamental" figure, caught between the testaments of Hebrew law and the good news of Jesus. John never surrenders his cry for repentance and purification by obedience to the law. He lays the ax at the root of the tree: Repent or know God's wrath! This approach is quite distinct from the message of Jesus, in which sin is met with forgiveness and salvation comes by way of faith, not moral perfection. Were Jesus and John merely playing "good cop, bad cop," or is there more to the discord between their proclamations?

We glimpse the struggle between the details. In Mark's early account, Jesus is baptized by John and may be a student of his for a time. He waits until John's arrest to take up his message of repentance for the coming kingdom. These details do not sit well with Matthew, who denies the implication that Jesus is ever in any way subordinate to John. Matthew adds John's protest at baptizing Jesus, professing unworthiness, and only Jesus' insistence that they enact this drama to fulfill God's purposes convinces him to follow through. Luke furthers the subordination of John in his infancy narratives, making sure John acknowledges the superiority of Jesus from the womb. Luke also reports John's arrest *before* the baptism of Jesus, as if to separate John from the event entirely.

We know that popular confusion between these two great figures continued at least through the end of the first century. In John's late Gospel, the baptism of Jesus is dispensed with altogether; Jesus is shown as promoting his own baptismal ministry—and he doesn't wait for John's arrest to do so (see John 4:1–3). When the Baptist gives witness to Jesus, he surrenders some of his own disciples and admits that as Jesus increases, his own influence must yield. Yet we are told in Acts that some communities are still baptizing in the name of John, as Apollos did. "Decreasing" the influence of John remained an issue in the early Church.

The same impulse that sought to level John the Baptist's stature throughout the era of gospel writing also worked on the Hellenists—those Greek-speaking Christians who posed some organizational trouble in the predominantly Hebrew-speaking Church of Jerusalem. Luke solves the problem expediently in Acts 6, showing how seven deacons are appointed to manage the interests of the Hellenists. Scholars wonder if perhaps the situation isn't being reported backwards: Did "the Seven" challenge the authority of the Apostles ("the Twelve") from the outset, and does Luke resolve the historical tension by presenting the Seven as serving at the *suggestion* of the Twelve rather than at loggerheads with it? If Luke's version of the story is to be taken at face value, then how are we to understand why Stephen, appointed as a deacon to distribute food so the Apostles are free to preach, ends up being martyred for preaching?

Finally, Luke works to modify the authority of James. No one disputes that James (not Zebedee's son but "the brother of the Lord," either kin to Jesus or a son of Joseph from an earlier marriage) was a significant leader in the Jerusalem Church. Some sources imply his influence even rivaled Peter's. A second-century gospel that did not make it into the canon shows Jesus bestowing his authority on James in a manner similar to the famous "thou art Peter" scene in Matthew 16. Even within the

New Testament in Acts, when Peter escapes from prison, he breathlessly orders: "Tell this to James and to the believers" (12:17). At the climactic Council of Jerusalem, it is James who renders the final judgment on what's to be done about the Gentile problem. When Paul goes up to Jerusalem before his arrest, he pays a visit to James and all the elders; Peter is not mentioned. (Paul confirms in Galatians that he met only with James.) Yet despite these clues to James' authority that slip into the account, Peter remains the dominant character in the Jerusalem Church according to Luke. Even the community that produces John's Gospel eventually capitulates to Peter's authority. Although evidence suggests they initially championed their own "beloved" founder as the premiere disciple, the later addition of John 21 shows how the beloved disciple, and John's community by extension, surrenders their rival claim to Peter in the end.

Managing Paul

Subordinating the influence of John the Baptist and James must have been child's play compared with the task of subjugating Paul. Paul was and remains a wildly charismatic, controversial, and powerful presence in Christianity. Some have suggested that Paul "invented" Christianity, at least as we know it today. It could be argued that if not for Paul's dogged insistence on proclaiming the gospel "to the ends of the earth," as Jesus once commanded, it might not have gotten much further than John the Baptist's movement did. Of course, other evidence indicates that inroads into the Gentile mission were originally made by Peter (see the story of the conversion of Cornelius in Acts 10-11). But Paul was the one willing to be stoned, imprisoned, and eventually put to death for defending the right of Gentiles to enjoy full membership in the Church. A good half of Acts is dedicated to the bold testimony and labor of this self-proclaimed Apostle.

There are, however, caveats to the story of Paul as told by Luke. Although in his letters Paul frequently calls himself an Apostle and defends himself against the "super apostles" of Jerusalem (see next chapter), Acts refrains from using this exclusive term in reference to Paul. Paul's own account of his dealings with headquarters in Jerusalem can be dismissive and even sarcastic. Yet in Acts he is portrayed as ever deferential to the Apostles.

The main source of this discrepancy remains the Council of Jerusalem as dually reported in Acts 15 and the Letter to the Galatians. Luke treats it as a sober ecclesial gathering: Paul and Barnabas voluntarily go up to Jerusalem to obtain a decision on what part of Jewish law, if any, Gentile Christians are bound to observe. The judgment is rendered in four parts, repeated often in Acts: 1) avoid meat sacrificed to idols, 2) avoid the meat of strangled animals, 3) avoid blood pollution, and 4) avoid unlawful marriage. When the ruling goes out in a letter from the Apostles, the proclamation begins "For it has seemed good to the Holy Spirit and to us to impose on you no further burden than these essentials" (15:28). The anvil of authority is heavy here, as when a Scripture professor of mine would underscore an argumentative point by declaring, "Jesus says ... and I tend to agree." Who could then argue?

Yet perhaps we should argue. In Galatians 2, Paul describes this same encounter as a simple private interview, one of those "courtesy calls" we are forced to make to the "powers that be." Paul reports that it was agreed that in return for allowing the Gentiles to join the Church without first becoming Jews he would ensure that the poor of Jerusalem should not be neglected. He then lambastes Peter (called Kephas or Cephas in Aramaic) for backtracking on the agreement later, going so far as to tell the Galatians, "I opposed him to his face, because he stood self-condemned" (Galatians 2:11). No wonder Paul's boldness caused shivers in Jerusalem and motivated Luke to subordinate Paul to Peter's authority at every narrative opportunity.

Contemporary Acts of the Church

The strain between *Petrine* and *Pauline* influences—those rooted in Peter or Paul respectively—continues to be felt in the Church today. Peter represents central authority, stability, and the power of the Church to teach and administrate; Petrine authority defines and codifies what it means to be Church—who's in,

57

who's out...and why. The Pauline impulse, by contrast, moves beyond legislation to embrace the freedom we receive by God's grace. The Pauline approach is comfortable entrusting believers with the decision of what to make of so great a gift. This fundamental difference of perception caused a rift in the Church at the time of the Reformation—and it still tugs at the heart of Christianity. Yet without both movements—to *conserve* and to *move beyond*—it is hard to imagine the Church at all.

Questions for Reflection and Discussion

1. Who are your heroes? What qualities make them heroic? How many of them might qualify as heroes in the tradition of the Church?

2. Consider the work of the Holy Spirit in Acts: proclamation, courage, healing, liberation and discernment. How many of them are present in your experience of Church today?

3. Luke speaks of a "golden age" of faith in the Church. What period of your life could be described as your spiritual "golden age"? What made it so?

4. How do you see authority and power operating in the Church today? How does it compare and contrast with the use of power in the secular world?

5. Review the influences of Peter and Paul on the early Church. How do you think Petrine and Pauline forces coexist in the Christian community today?

Faith Response

Seek the release of the Holy Spirit's gifts in your life. Exercise discernment instead of simply making decisions. Be courageous in doing the right thing. Be a healing and liberating presence in the lives of those around you.

Letters Written on the Heart

I have a batch of old letters that I will never throw away, no matter how many times I move or how tight storage space gets. Those letters are important because of who wrote them, the time of life I received them, or the particular message they bear for me. This bundle of paper is precious because it reminds me that I have been found worthy of love and friendship. Some of their lines I have read so many times that I can close my eyes and recite them from memory.

I'm not the only one with these kinds of treasures. When friends and loved ones have died, I've gone through their possessions to find that many of them also have a letter or boxes of letters that they could never bear to part with. (I suppose the next generation will have their letters in a file on their hard drive.) These written words have the power to crystallize a relationship. They dare to speak a truth and thus move us deeply because they were meant for us personally. Unlike the volume of words that pass before our eyes each day at work or in the newspaper, the words of a letter speak right to our hearts.

Ancient Letters

While e-mail has revolutionized the style of our letter writing, correspondence has retained its various grades of formality and informality. Unlike electronic mail, which often dispenses with greetings and salutations and thus becomes more like a conversation in progress, we still follow standard conventions of correspondence when we take pen to paper: "Dear Tom" and "Best wishes to you and the kids."

Ancient letters had their degrees of formality as well. The twenty-one letters that appear in the New Testament are often generically identified as *epistles*, a very formal kind of letter that was read or circulated publicly. Epistles were self-conscious literature; that is, they were intended to be "published," like an essay or a proclamation. In this sense, less than half of the New Testament letters qualify as epistles. Except for possibly the Letter to the Romans, none of Paul's letters were epistles in the classic sense.

Nor could they be categorized as private correspondence. For example, although Paul wrote to Philemon personally, even that letter contains greetings for the rest of his household (although I suppose that could fall under "Best wishes to you and the church"). The Letter to Philemon concerns the very delicate business of how to receive a runaway slave, yet Paul speaks both intimately and instructively to Philemon, never entirely surrendering his status as teacher. Overall, Paul's letters are not quite epistles, yet they certainly are more than postcards from his missionary journeys. Scholars prefer to call them "apostolic letters." This recognition of his apostleship would have pleased Paul—although he doubtless would have censored his letters had he dreamed they would wind up as Scripture one day!

An ancient letter had its stylistic conventions: a greeting, which could be quite long; the body of the message; and a final greeting and signature. An optional thanksgiving might follow the original greeting in Roman usage, although not in Jewish custom. Paul's letters exemplify these conventions, and they generally include a thanksgiving. He also adds a blessing at the end of many of his letters. In between, Paul divides his message between expounding on doctrine—the unity of the Church, the saving power of Jesus Christ—and giving pastoral advice on specific matters.

But a letter from Paul can contain a whole lot more: hymns, homilies, liturgical formulas from an already established Christian ritual, or household codes of behavior lifted from secular sources and given a Christian twist. Paul is also not above pleading, cajoling, threatening, praising, boasting and blaming. He can be sublime, as in his poetic reflection on the nature of love ("Love is patient; love is kind," 1 Corinthians 13:4) or downright insulting ("You foolish Galatians!" "I wish those who unsettle you would castrate themselves!" Galatians 3:1, 5:12). Paul isn't consciously auditioning for the Bible. He is just trying to communicate—or, in his words, he is trying to be "all things to all people" (1 Corinthians 9:22). Whatever it takes to get his point across is fair game to Paul.

Who Wrote Paul's Letters?

Asking this question is not the same as asking "Who's buried in Grant's tomb?" When we talk about ancient texts, authorship is always a question to be asked—and a hard one to answer. Thirteen or fourteen letters in the New Testament are traditionally attributed to Paul (the fourteenth being the Letter to the Hebrews), but even early on the church fathers debated which of the letters were actually authored by Paul. If you read Bible scholarship of the nineteenth century, you might conclude that almost none of the Pauline letters are Paul's. Today, however, there is general agreement that seven letters—1 Thessalonians, Galatians, Philippians, 1 and 2 Corinthians, Romans, and Philemon—are authentically his. Another three—2 Thessalonians, Colossians, and Ephesians—are considered *Deutero-Pauline* (which means they are derived from Paul's ideas and possibly written by a student of his). However, the three pastoral letters—1 and 2 Timothy and Titus—are much later in origin and bear a different style and focus. So the scorecard for the letters reads: seven genuinely Paul's, three related to his ideas, three almost certainly not his. As for the Letter to the Hebrews, the consensus is that it belongs in another category entirely. (See the next chapter on the "catholic" letters.)

From here, the waters get a little muddier. In some letters we note references to other correspondence that never made it into the canon. For example, the letters to the Corinthians refer to previous letters to the community that we don't have. Also, a careful reading of 1 Thessalonians, Philippians, and 2 Corinthians shows seams in the organization of their ideas that suggest they may be compiled fragments of several separate exchanges.

Finally, the definition of authorship in Paul's time was not as clear-cut as it is now. It was accepted practice to sign a letter that: a) you wrote yourself, b) you dictated word by word to someone else, c) you outlined to a scribe who was responsible for the composition, d) you commissioned a scribe to write entirely. It has been argued that all thirteen of the Pauline letters could be explained in this way: Paul wrote or dictated seven himself; he collaborated with a scribe on three more; he was old or sick and therefore delegated responsibility for the so-called pastorals to someone else. In any case, if you want to get a feel for what is purely Paul's expression, first read the undisputed seven. If you go on to read the others later, you'll experience the perceptible change in style, tone, and subject matter that scholars are talking about.

In any case, the six pseudo-Pauline letters written in his name aren't technical forgeries. Disciples sought to honor a teacher by writing in his name and extending his school of thought. Arguably, the audience that received the later letters would have known they were not literally from Paul—he may have been dead when they were produced. However, the community would have appreciated that Paul's authority was being invoked in the teachings. Our inclusion of these letters as inspired teachings in our Scripture means we appreciate that too.

How to Read Paul

The order of Paul's letters in the New Testament is not necessarily a suggestion as to how they should be read. Rather, the organization of the letters in most Christian Bibles is based on the principle of *stichometry* (a word you will have little use for unless you organize your bills this way: it means longest comes first). The letters of Paul are organized by length and not chronology.

However, if you'd like to read the letters in the order they were *written*, to get the sense of Paul's maturing ideas, attempts have been made to date them. The order is presumed to be from the first century A.D. as follows:

c. 51: 1 Thessalonians
c. 54: Galatians
c. 57: 1 and 2 Corinthians, Philemon, Philippians
c. 58: Romans

If Paul had a hand in 2 Thessalonians, Colossians, and Ephesians as well, he wrote them from prison in Rome between 61 and 63. If he authored the pastoral letters, it would have been after he was released from prison (if he ever was), between 64 and 68. (See Paul's story below for this debate.) The early Church put Titus before Timothy's letters, if that helps you get organized further.

Paul's Story

Without question, Paul's effect on the history of Christianity is profound. If there's one thinker after Jesus whose imprint on the Church is greater than Paul's, he or she hasn't been born yet. Paul has been called the architect of the Church; religious skeptics have even called him the inventor of the Church. Although the "chair of authority" went to Peter, Paul's teachings became Scripture, which gives him the last word in the unique sense that it would take a shrewd pope or church council to get past a doctrinal cornerstone laid by Paul.

How did Paul get to be so huge? After all, he wasn't one of the Twelve, and there is no evidence that he met Jesus before the crucifixion. Yet Paul was a key catch in the "people fishing" that the Apostles were sent to accomplish—although as grace would have it they didn't really catch him, Jesus did. (If they *had* caught Paul immediately after he had led the persecution of the early Church, the last thing on their minds might have been his conversion!) From the start, Paul was trouble, and even after his baptism he never seemed to get out of hot water with the others.

So here's the "skinny" on Paul. He was probably born the year after Jesus in the city of Tarsus (a better address than Nazareth if you're looking for opportunity). Tarsus was a well-known cultural center of Asia Minor, visited by the likes of Julius Caesar and Cleopatra. The citizens of Tarsus had been granted Roman citizenship by Mark Antony; so under the law Paul, a Jew, was also Roman. This fact saved his neck on more than one occasion.

Paul was not simply a Jew, however. He was a *Hellenized* Jew. This means he grew up outside of Israel and was part of the *diaspora*, those "dispersed" Jews who chose not to live in the promised land. Hellenization brought with it the Greek language, education, and advantages to citizens of the empire. But it was regarded with suspicion by the people in the provinces, intent as they were on maintaining their language, values, and way of life. Citizens of Jerusalem, as Scripture witnesses, did not care much for the Greek-speaking Jews. In Acts, we get a sense of the antagonism between the Hellenists and the Hebrew-speaking Jews among the first Christian converts. Both in Acts and in Paul's letters, we see clear evidence that Paul's credibility with the Jerusalem Christians was never very good.

Yet Acts tells us that Paul was schooled in Hebrew theology in Jerusalem as a student of the famous rabbi Gamaliel. Paul doesn't mention this, but he does insist he was a strictly observant Pharisee with great zeal for the Jewish law. He must have had contacts in high places, for he received papers to seize Christians on behalf of the Sanhedrin. His prestige or notoriety as a persecutor of Christians—depending on your viewpoint—was such that his name was as feared among Christians as it was celebrated among traditionally-minded Jews. Then came the great reversal.

The story of Paul's conversion is told many times in Acts, and Paul alludes to it in his letters as well. He insists he encountered the risen Lord as literally as did the women and the Twelve at Easter. In this revelation, Jesus both accused and commissioned Paul. This is why Paul feels justified later in calling himself an apostle ("one sent"), a title otherwise reserved for the Twelve.

At first, the Christians find it hard to trust that Paul isn't out to betray them. At the same time, the Jerusalem authorities are outraged that Paul the Pharisee has joined the Jesus camp. Later, the Christians accept Paul's conversion but remain leery of his vehement mission to the Gentiles. Jewish Christians hound his mission churches, debunking his teaching and his authority. Paul has face-offs with Peter and receives curt instructions from James. He will have differences of opinion with his companion missionaries, Barnabas and John Mark, and his established churches are always softly crumbling into dissent and confusion behind him. Yet, through this atmosphere of mistrust and friction, with a remarkable lack of support from every quarter, Paul remains true to his inner conviction that Jesus has sent him to bring the good news to the Gentiles. And largely through his efforts, that gospel spreads through the ancient world.

So what happened to Paul at the end of the story? Acts doesn't tell us, ending with Paul's imprisonment in Rome, which Luke reports lasted two full years. Paul had hoped to go to Spain after his last ill-fated journey to Jerusalem, but instead he fell into the hands of the Jewish authorities who felt betrayed by his conversion. They turned him over to the Roman officials, who allowed him to languish in prison—first in Caesarea 58 through 60, then in Rome, under house arrest from 61 to 63. Some presume that Paul was tried, sentenced, and killed in Rome shortly thereafter. Others disagree. Clement of Rome (c. 95) says Paul was tried, released, and made it to Spain to begin his European mission. A writer around 180 claims to have seen a manuscript of Acts with the "missing" ending intact, describing Paul's departure for Spain. Eusebius (c. third century) writes simply that Paul was martyred by Nero sometime between 64 and 68. Dionysius (c. second century) reports that Paul was martyred along with Peter, which would place the date near 65. Tertullian (c. second century) adds that Paul was beheaded, like John the Baptist (as a Roman citizen, he could not be crucified). Did Paul make it to Spain? Did he return later to Rome to be martyred? We do know that Constantine built a basilica over Paul's remains in Rome. The rest is hearsay.

The Gospel According to Paul

Paul used his biography freely in his preaching. His story is, in a vital way, part of his message. It must have seemed to his old friends at the Sanhedrin that Paul had become a heretic. In a bitter twist of history, Paul's words were later misused in the cause of anti-Semitism, which would have horrified him. The truth is, Paul never repudiated his Judaism, nor did he ever encourage any Jew to do so. Rather, Paul remained theologically grounded in the God of Hebrew Scripture and tradition.

What changed for Paul was not his *theology* (that is, his view of God) but his *Christology* (his understanding of the *Messiah* or Christ, a purely Jewish concept). Embracing the crucified Jesus as the Christ of God was "a stumbling block" to the Jewish mind, as Paul freely admits. A crucified man was accursed according to Hebrew teaching, and that settled the issue for many Jews who otherwise admired Jesus during his ministry. Paul was able to see his way past that obstacle, however, declaring that the "curse" had become a "blessing" by the power of God. This new vision further enabled him to see death as the door to new life, weakness as the perfection of power, and suffering as the pathway to glory. Paul's grasping of the paradox of Jesus became his gospel, and the natural outcome of this paradox is that outsiders were now invited in. The Gentiles were welcome to share in the salvation of the Jews.

The cross, however, remained the stumbling block to faith in Jesus for traditional Jews. But Jewish Christians overcame that obstacle to face another, more subtle one—the requirement of Jewishness. Perhaps they could accept that Jesus invited Gentiles to the party, but wasn't it obvious they had to come *all the way in*, i.e., they had to become circumcised and law-abiding Jews? The written record reveals an uncertain policy in this regard. In Acts 16, for example, Luke claims that Paul had his companion Timothy circumcised to appease the Jews of Lyconia. But in Galatians 2, Paul resists circumcising fellow missionary Titus. Did Paul waver on this issue, or is Acts 16 another example of Luke's role as reconciler?

A man in Timothy or Titus's position may have had more at stake in this bit of legislation than we do today. But to Paul, it involved a slippery slope of logic that ended in the utter repudiation of Christ. You believe that salvation comes either from Christ or from the law of Israel, demonstrated in circumcision. If your trust is in the law, obviously you don't need Christ. If you don't need Christ, what are you doing in the Christian community to begin with? History, we can see, sided with Paul.

The idea that Christ is bigger than the law is often viewed as the essence of Paul's teaching. In the sixteenth century, the motto of the Protestant Reformation was "justification by faith in Christ and not in the law" (which would have saved Timothy some hardship). But to the Reformers, Paul's teaching also countered the established Church of Rome and its use of any form of "mediating" grace, including sacraments, good works, obedience, or the offering of prayer—all seen to dilute or contradict the saving power of Christ. By the nineteenth century, a millennial interest in Paul took another shift. The emphasis was now on the apocalyptic choice between this world and the one to come. Others embraced Paul's writings as a kind of Christian mysticism in which communion with the risen Lord was accomplished by baptism and celebrated in Eucharist. Branches of Christianity have been founded on one or another of Paul's ideas, all of them sound elements of Christian faith.

In the twentieth century, theologians focused on the Pauline principle of "decision." You make your decision for Christ or for the world. Jesus either is or is not your Savior—and if you decide for Jesus, yours is the mystery of revelation, the transforming power of the Spirit, the promises of God's ancient covenant, and the universal communion of the saints in this world and the next. Any other decision would be fatal. Because it is "in Christ"—a phrase Paul uses 165 times in his undisputed letters—we are justified (acquitted from past sin), reconciled (made one with God), and redeemed (rescued from the consequences of sin and death).

Some have wondered if this means that being saved by Christ cancels any further obligation to be, in a word, "good." But Paul says that our faith must be worked out in love (see Galatians 5:6). Or, as Protestant theologian Rudolf Bultmann put it, "You are a justified Christian, so live like one!" Paul could not have said it better.

Questions for Reflection and Discussion

1. Describe letters, poems, quotations or books that have been significant for you. Recall one or two banners, plaques or bumper stickers that express words you live by.

2. How do you communicate your deepest thoughts and feelings to others (e-mail, letters, phone calls, heart-to-heart

and face-to-face talks, crafts, cooking)? How does the form of your expression shape what gets expressed?

3. Which aspects of Paul's story seem most familiar in comparison with yours? Which seem most remote? What do you admire most about Paul? Why?

4. Is faith in Jesus "enough," or do you think the practice of religion needs more to work with than a declaration of faith? Explain your answer.

5. At which moments in your life, sacramental or personal, did you feel like you were making a decision for Christ? How did those moments change you?

Faith Response

Make a decision, prayerfully and seriously, about whether you can accept Jesus—cross and all—as the Way, the Truth, and the Life. Consider how this commitment affects your relationships, the way you live, the decisions you make, and what you do with your time.

The Epistles of James, Peter, John, Jude,
and the Letter to the Hebrews

Church:
The Next Generation

In the modern world, travel has become a way of life and, at times, a necessary evil. Business trips, holiday visits back to the hometown, and vacations involve hours spent on the move. Motel beds or the guest futon become part of the sense of upheaval and strangeness. That's why many of us look for familiar haunts to make us feel at home, no matter what city we're in. Such institutions ease the discomfort of displacement with warm feelings of belonging. For me, the House of Blues is like that. Whether you're in Chicago or New Orleans or Anaheim, the House of Blues manages to deliver the same wonderful food, terrific atmosphere, great music, and fun service people. Of course, there is something to be said for being open to new experiences, and I'm not averse to broadening my horizons. But suppertime is not the hour I'm looking for adventure.

The essential blessing of any institution is the production of a stable, reliable, repeatable experience. It's something you can count on to remain constant in its core identity and appeal. Although local variations are to be expected, I know the jambalaya and rosemary cornbread will always be waiting for me at the House of Blues.

The Institution of the Church
Institution is a cold-sounding word. We think at once of banks and corporations, government agencies, large universities and hospitals, and other long-standing structures that may not always have the interests of the little individual at heart. When we speak of the Church as an institution, some conjure up twenty centuries of machinery geared primarily to maintain

itself. But institutions are not fundamentally heartless entities; they are a useful, even necessary component of survival. If something valuable is to be transported from today into tomorrow, an institution is just the vehicle to deliver it.

Institutions provide identity, promote belonging, safeguard goals, nurture growth, and foster maturity. These were issues for the early Church as it considered how to convey the *deposit of faith*—those truths it had received from a generation fading in the rearview mirror—to generations yet unborn. Originally, people thought Jesus' return in glory would happen in their lifetime. As years passed and this expectation was not realized, however, they started to form an organization that would support the ongoing mission of the Church to spread the good news.

As we have seen, the first step in getting organized was to compile the stories about Jesus—teachings, sayings and memories—into the written texts of the Gospels. Church leaders also gathered the letters of Paul as valuable reflections on salvation, the Church, the Holy Spirit, as well as useful pastoral strategies for common local problems. They developed prayers, rituals and hymns, enabling each local community to worship with a sense of unity as the Body of Christ. They organized roles of responsibility and accountability—what we know today as the *hierarchy* of leadership. All of this structure helped to preserve what became known as the *catholicity*, or universal character, of the Church. And back then, without the convenience of telephone and Internet, the means of keeping the whole institution integrated involved the written word, primarily in the form of the epistle.

The epistle, we noted, differs from Paul's apostolic letters in that it is an intentionally open letter to the whole Church, formal in style and subject, a conscious official document rather than a personal address. (When our present-day pope or bishops want to communicate with the whole Church, they use essentially the same method in *encyclicals* and *pastoral letters* respectively.) The remaining letters of the New Testament are largely epistolary in form. They are often grouped together under the name *catholic letters*, a term first used by the church fathers. Of course, the Roman Catholic Church as we know it today was not imagined at the time this phrase was first used. But by the end of the first century, Ignatius of Antioch was speaking of the Christian community as "catholic"—that is, universal and united in faith. Because the catholic letters had authority throughout the various local communities, they are titled by their author rather than their audience, as Paul's were. According to Eusebius, seven epistles were included among the catholic letters by the second century: one by James, two by Peter, three by John, and one by Jude.

The Source of the Catholic Letters
As a warning, let me say that this section will be unsatisfying to anyone who likes straight answers to simple questions. It's tempting to respond as Origen did in the third century when asked about the author of the Letter to the Hebrews: "God knows." The accumulation of scholarship on these letters is impressive only to the degree that it reaches a grand lack of consensus on nearly every aspect of dating and authorship. So use a mental pencil with a big eraser when making note of the following information.

The only two of these letters accepted into the canon of Scripture without much protest were 1 Peter and 1 John. The rest were heatedly debated, some for centuries; Jude got in last, and by a hair, in the fourth century. It seemed clear to the church fathers, at least, that 1 Peter and 1 John might have been written by the men whose names they bear, but the rest were of doubtful origin. In later centuries, even those two letters would be up for debate. Today it is commonly held that all of the catholic letters may be *pseudonymous* (written under an assumed name). However, you'll always find a scholar willing to prove the minority opinion that some or all of them could have been written by their namesakes, if we are but willing to engage in enough theoretical gymnastics.

The commonly presumed chronological order of these letters is: 1 Peter, James, Jude, Hebrews, 1, 2 and 3 John, and 2 Peter. (Hebrews is sometimes thrown in with the catholic letters for want of a better place to put it, just as John's letters are often included in discussions of John's Gospel or the Book of Revelation.) These works are ordered in our Bibles quite differently for reasons that are not clear. (The biblical order has been linked to a stray reference in Galatians 2:9 to an established series— "James and Peter and John"—which seems a real stretch.) Although our present biblical order places Paul's writings before the catholic letters, earlier arrangements put the catholic letters ahead of Paul's, establishing a greater prestige for the purported works by Apostles. (Once again, Paul's self-proclaimed apostleship took a backseat.) Since the catholic letters share a sense of central church organization with the Acts of the Apostles, they also may have seemed to follow that book naturally. The Letter to the Hebrews, which has more in common with the catholic letters than the apostolic letters of Paul, is placed between Paul's corpus and the other epistles.

But if the authorship and ordering of the letters is unclear, frankly so is the idea that all of these epistles are "catholic." 1 Peter and the latter two letters of John are addressed to specific communities, not to the whole Church. What's more, some of the letters lack an address or other recognizable letter conventions. Hebrews, most notably, is not a letter at all but more like a sermon or treatise, and 2 and 3 John are letters but do not qualify as classic epistles.

The only thing certain about these documents is that whoever wrote them and whenever they were written, Jude preceded 2 Peter. If you read Jude first and then read 2 Peter, you immediately see that 2 Peter is an expanded and edited version of Jude. It may not be much to hold on to during a discussion of sources, but biblical scholarship has been built on thinner reeds than this.

Because this section of the New Testament has so little obvious unity, I'd like to discuss these documents separately.

James, Paul and Martin Luther

James *is* a catholic letter in more ways than one. Martin Luther and other Protestant reformers rejected this letter in the sixteenth century because of its stance on the relationship between faith and works (see James 2:14–18). The idea that our actions ("works") are integral to God's work of salvation in us was repugnant to the reformers. They took Paul's theology to heart that we are all sinners who are "justified" (acquitted of sin) by faith in Jesus Christ and not by our own efforts. "Justification by faith" (and not by works) became the rallying cry of generations of Protestants, who labeled their Catholic cousins as believers in a salvation that could be bought or earned by doing good works. Catholics, for their part, stereotyped Protestants as those who gave lip service to the declaration of faith and did not take as seriously the mandate to live what they professed.

These mutually disparaging stereotypes persisted for four hundred years, and only recently, in the *Joint Declaration on the Doctrine of Justification,* labored over by both Catholic and Lutheran theologians since 1967 and signed in 1998, was the matter put to rest. Who "won" the debate, Protestants or Catholics, faith or works? Actually, James won the argument. He was the first to translate Paul's insistence that faith must be worked out in love (Galatians 5:6) into the well-known formula that faith without works is dead (see James 2:17). So the answer to the centuries-long contest is that, yes, we are saved by God's initiative alone, but a people who know they are saved by love will respond with love. So as James says, "Show me your faith apart from your works, and I by my works will show you my faith" (2:18).

The Letter of James has other controversies attached to it, mostly involving internal features. For one thing, the letter mentions the name of Jesus only twice, and the content overall concerns ethics and morality. It is strikingly similar to Hebrew wisdom literature of the previous century (see Sirach, Proverbs, Wisdom of Solomon in the Old Testament), which makes scholars wonder if the letter is not simply a Jewish homily that has been "baptized" by the insertion of Jesus' name. (The Jewish-sounding address to "the twelve tribes of the dispersion" could be an artful reference to the "new Israel" of the Church, but it also sounds like a reference to those Jews living outside of Israel.) This theory is countered by those who point to the inclusion of a section in James on healing and the confession of sin, unknown in Jewish tradition (see James 5:13–16). If James was based on a work from the Hebrew wisdom tradition, the writer did more than add the name of Jesus twice.

The author of James seems to have been familiar with Matthew's Gospel and may have based part of his letter on the Sermon on the Mount. This leads scholars to date James no earlier than the 80s. Others put the date as late as the 90s because of James' often-declared opposition of "the world" to God, an idea crucial to John's Gospel of that later decade. Of course, those who maintain that James the writer is also "the brother of the Lord" (despite his excellent Greek, rare for a Galilean) date it around the year of James' death, 62.

Peter, Paul and Isaiah

If either of the letters attributed to Peter are from his hand, it could only be the first one. At least that letter might have been based on Peter's ideas and developed by a scribe who spoke good Greek and had a fine knowledge of Hebrew Scripture— neither of which Peter the fisherman is known to have possessed. What really troubles scholars, though, is that 1 Peter is addressed to the churches of Asia Minor—Paul's mission territory. Why, when Paul was still alive (remember, they were martyred at roughly the same time), would Peter be writing to Paul's communities?

If Peter did initiate this letter, it would be dated around the year of his death, 65. If a student of Peter wrote it, the suggestions range from the 70s to the 90s. Since 1 Peter shows some dependence on Pauline thought, it was likely written after Paul's letters were circulating broadly in a collection. The author writes about a trial by fire (see 4:12) that may allude to the persecutions prominent toward the end of the century. He also addresses those who are "aliens and exiles" (2:11) in the world, an attitude late-century Christians adopted as society became increasingly hostile to their otherworldly ideals. Since 1 Peter is a letter about the need to give good witness, we should note that the word for *witness* is the same for *martyr* in Greek. A martyr's primary task was to testify to the faith, to the point of death.

In addition, 1 Peter contains an extensive reflection on Christian baptism and, despite a keen awareness of death, is characterized by the spirit of hope. It compares the saving power of baptism to the ark of Noah that lifted his family away from the destruction brought on by human sinfulness. The letter urges believers to allow themselves to be built into a spiritual house as "living stones"—reminiscent of Jesus, the cornerstone once rejected (see 2:4–8). The underlying theology of hope in spite of suffering is a kind of meditation on Isaiah 53, one of the servant songs that parallels Jesus' understanding of a messiah who must suffer. The bloodiness of this letter may seem appalling to modern sensibilities, but the writer emphasizes that the blood of Jesus was not shed to placate a severe God but to bond us to God in the manner of a covenant sign. So 1 Peter redefines Christian hope not as passive optimism in a better future but as hope-in-action, the only appropriate lifestyle for the end times.

Hebrews and the Humanity of Jesus

By any measure, the Letter to the Hebrews is unique in the New Testament. A sermon more than a letter, it translates the passion of Jesus from an earthly event into a heavenly liturgical action. It reminds us that—to a priestly people like ourselves (see 1 Peter 2:9)—all of life *is* worship, and so, in a unique way, is the death of every Christian. Chapter 5 of Hebrews reveals a tender portrait of how Jesus suffered in the hour of his betrayal, sharing our fear of death and the agony of our surrender. The theology of hope and sacrifice closely resembles 1 Peter; however, instead of identifying the blood of Christ as a covenant sign, Hebrews reminds us that the word *sacrifice* means "to make holy." The sacrifice of Jesus consecrated the whole world. This exhortation was meant to bolster the faith of Jewish Christians who were losing fervor in the ongoing hardship of Christian living.

Speculation has identified the author of the letter as Barnabas or Apollos or Priscilla, all fellow missionaries at the time of Paul. The evidence neither denies nor confirms those guesses. Hebrews is generally dated between 80 and 90. It is written in the best Greek of the New Testament, and its compelling theme—intercession as a means of sanctifying the world—is an affirmation of our common vocation to lift up the world in our prayer.

One John or Many?

The source of the writings attributed to John—including the Gospel, three letters, and the Book of Revelation—have long been a puzzle. Are they all by one hand? Many scholars today believe the Gospel of John was written by a school that formed around a central figure possibly represented by "the beloved disciple" mentioned in the story. The variant endings of John's Gospel in the early manuscripts imply at least an editor's hand. The letters of John were probably produced by the same community, possibly written by one person—although not necessarily the same person responsible for the bulk of the Gospel. But the narrator of Revelation, John of Patmos, is most likely a separate author, and none of these "Johns" is identified with the son of Zebedee by the same name. The letters were probably written between 90 and 100.

The unity of the disciples was a concern in John's Gospel of the same period, and we glimpse the reason in the letters. The community is fracturing, and bitterness is increasing among the factions. We hear the themes of the Gospel echoed here—the opposing forces of light and darkness, the importance of witnesses, and the fullness of joy that is known in unity. But joy may be at a premium, since the community is at odds with some of its teachers who have come to be known as "enemies," "deceivers" and "antichrists." In 2 John, the author warns that these people should not be admitted to the assembly or even greeted (see v.10), and 3 John sadly reveals that legitimate missionaries sent by the leader of the community are not being received. It is a difficult time for John's assembly.

What is notably lacking in these epistles is a connection between this assembly and the *episcopacy* (shepherd authority) invested in Peter and administered in this generation by Clement. We know from Clement's extra-biblical writing that lines of authority in the Church were still being consolidated at century's end. John's community was one of the last to capitulate their special insular tradition to external leadership. The letters of John, written in the same period as the first draft of John's Gospel, seem to overlook the primacy of Peter in favor of their leader. The addition of chapter 21 to John's Gospel, however, can be read as evidence that sometime after the fracturing of John's community the remainder accepted Peter's line of authority as final.

Jude, Peter and Enoch
One commentator has called Jude and 2 Peter the least studied part of the New Testament. People may feel justified in skipping Jude, at least, because it is so esoteric. In a mere twenty-five verses, it manages to lose the casual reader in short order—unless he or she has a good set of footnotes. But for this same reason, Jude is fascinating to students of the Bible. What scholars recognize in reading Jude is its generous use of Hebrew writings that do not appear in our Old Testament—books like *The Assumption of Moses* and *The Book of Enoch*. (Enoch is a minor character in Scripture—see Genesis 5:21-24—but his legend is large in outside writings and praised by Sirach and Hebrews within the Bible as well.) Jude's liberal use of outside sources is a clue that it was written before the Jewish Bible (our Old Testament) was definitively set in 100 A.D. Jude's recollection of the Apostles as past heroes of the faith, and its reference to "the faith" as a set of doctrines already formally established, confirms a late-century date. Some have mistaken this Jude for Jude Thaddeus the Apostle, but this Jude calls himself "brother of James," who is likewise called "brother of the Lord." This would make Jude a relative of Jesus, thought scholars believe his survival to the date this letter was written is unlikely.

Jude stresses the importance of memory. He expresses the Jewish idea that to sin is to forget God. Therefore, remembering the past is the best insurance against temptation in the present, especially in the presence of false teachers. His argument is attractive enough in the early Church to warrant a "rerun" in 2 Peter. The author of this second letter attributed to Peter takes the Letter of Jude and subtracts the references to non-biblical material and adds biblical examples. He is specific about the heresy of the false teachers, which remained vague in Jude. In 2 Peter, those teachers are said to deny that Christ will ever return in glory, since he hadn't shown up after all this time. The author's reply is familiar to most Christians: "With the Lord one day is like a thousand years, and a thousand years are like one day" (2 Peter 3:8) He reminds us that what we await are "new heavens and a new earth, where righteousness is at home" (3:13).

Since 2 Peter makes use of Jude's letter but rejects the material excluded from the canon in the year 100, dating has been suggested between 100 and 140. This would preclude Peter or any of his immediate associates as the author.

The End (of the World)
One thing is clear from reading the work of second-generation Christians. They were really anxious for the world to end. Those early Christians shared with us an emotional attachment to loved ones and to the beauty of the natural world. To them, however, the end of the world was less about destruction than it was about the vindication of their hope. The return of Jesus in glory would be proof that their faith was not in vain. Also, the glorious Second Coming would usher in a new age, a "new creation" that would resemble the original handiwork of God in blessing, wholeness and goodness. It would retire the "old creation" which had fallen prey to sin, sadness and so much suffering. It would put an end to death and be a source of joy to all who longed for its coming. (For more about the end—and the new beginning—read the next chapter on the Book of Revelation.)

Questions for Reflection and Discussion

1. Where do you seek the comfort of stability and familiarity? Which organizations, rituals or habits are "institutions" in your life?

2. What are some elements of "catholicity"—the Church's universal character—that hold the Church together today? Which are indispensable to the Church in every age?

3. Identify some characteristics of hierarchy and authority in government, business, community and family. How does the Church's hierarchy exercise authority in ways that are the same? Different?

4. How do the dual elements of faith and good works play a role in your life as a Christian? Do you think one is more important than the other? Explain your answer.

5. Do you think Christians should be "strangers and sojourners" (as in 1 Peter 2:11) in the world? How does your faith set you apart from the world? How does it enmesh you in the world in a deeper way?

Faith Response

Consider which aspect of your Christianity is weaker: your development in faith or your practice of good works. Decide on three concrete ways you can begin to bolster that weaker side as a disciple of Jesus.

The Fifth Gospel?

Guessing games are fine for parties, but few people like to guess when it comes to moral decision-making. When dealing with right and wrong, many of us prefer clarity and certainty to the morass of ambiguous choices we often face. We appreciate the poetic truth spoken in Ecclesiastes: "For everything there is a season, and a time for every matter under heaven" (3:1), but what we really want to know is how to tell *when* it's time for war or time for peace; time for mending or time for tearing; time for uprooting or time for planting; time for silence or time for speaking out.

When confronted with distressing uncertainties in making choices today, many of us turn to religion for help. We expect our faith to provide answers, or at least some criteria by which we can arrive at our own answers. Many of us view religious beliefs as guides or tools, but not as replacements for the personal responsibility that results from free will. Others, however, approach religion as the direct expression of God's will, a set of rules to be incorporated and obeyed to the letter. When people employ religious teaching and especially Scripture in this black-and-white, literal way, we describe them as religious *fundamentalists*. The fundamentalist approach divides human reality into unambiguous sectors of good and evil, right and wrong, true and false. It relegates free will to a single choice: to accept God's way or to reject it. Fundamentalism outlines the stark consequences of choosing for or against God. It promotes crystal moral clarity and is especially attractive to people who live in troubled and confusing circumstances.

Perhaps this is why fundamentalists of every era—including our own—are fascinated by the Book of Revelation. The last book of the Bible outlines in vivid terms what happens to those who side with or against God in the end. But is this all the book does, and is that what it was intended to do?

A View from the Apocalypse

To read the Book of Revelation thoughtfully, it helps to know something about the style in which the book is written. Revelation is an example of *apocalyptic* writing, a word that means "unveiling." (The book is alternately called the Apocalypse for that reason.) Apocalyptic literature was originally an extension of the prophetic tradition and was common in Hebrew and Christian writings between 200 B.C. and 200 A.D. Classical prophets understood their primary responsibility as interpreting their own times in light of God's word. But the prophetic role gradually incorporated that of the seer, one who revealed future consequences as well. Examples of apocalyptic writing in the Bible include passages from Daniel, Ezekiel, Isaiah, Joel and other prophets. Jesus and Saint Paul also occasionally employed apocalyptic images to capture the religious imagination of their audiences.

Apocalyptic literature is very stylized. It typically includes a tour of heaven or hell and makes great use of angels, cosmic books, symbolic numbers, allegory, and allusions to contemporary references familiar to its intended audience. As a literature of "unveiling," it is couched in "hidden" terms not fully accessible to the hearer. Apocalypse affords a glimpse of heaven's ultimate designs, but doesn't spell out a one-to-one correspondence in the details. Instead, it offers symbolic language to encourage further reflection.

When we read Revelation today, we may conclude that such works are remarkably dark and negative in focus—all that destruction visited upon the earth and its inhabitants! It might surprise us that the original intent of apocalyptic writing was to comfort believers in times of distress and motivate them to recommit fervently to the cause. God will triumph, the message of apocalypse says plainly. The excitation of fear and strong emotion that such writing could elicit was deliberate. Its message was clear for those losing heart or sitting on the fence: Now is the time to get up and take a stand.

If you resist negativity in religion, you may protest that the fear of punishment is a lousy way to sell people on faith in God. Admittedly, plenty of punishment is handed out in Revelation, and you don't want to be counted among God's enemies when the stars fall to the earth and the sky is dark with locusts. Putting the details of punishment aside, consider the proposition that actions have consequences. The bottom line of apocalyptic thought is that we must take active responsibility for our choices. The reality of unpleasant consequences motivates us every day to do lots of things we'd rather not do: exercise, brush our teeth, study for tests, upkeep home repairs. If we fail to do these things, is it God's wrath if we reap what our omissions sow? The world bears the sad mark of human sinfulness and, like us, is marked for death. Time itself will foreclose, and the world will pass away. If we become allied with what is not lasting, we will ultimately lose everything.

The Timing of Revelation

Some originally assumed the Apostle John wrote Revelation. Of the five works attributed to John, it is the only one that actually bore the name John in the manuscript. But its late dating, around 95 A.D., eliminates that identification. Zebedee's son John was martyred before the year 70, according to tradition. Thus, scholars now presume John of Patmos was another fellow entirely. He is no longer commonly identified with the writer of the Gospel or the letters of John. This writer's Greek is the poorest in the New Testament—as one scholar put it, he thinks in Hebrew but writes in barbaric Greek.

Rome bears the brunt of this writer's scorn—whether because of Christian persecution or for the usual glaring sins of empire is hard to say. He equates Rome with Babylon—in Hebrew tradition the great pagan empire responsible for destroying the original Temple (as Rome did the second one) and keeping the faithful in exile (which is precisely how Christians felt as aliens in civil culture). Rome is described as a great whore, seducing the body of the faithful to forswear Christ and to join with her corruption instead. It is no accident that the mark of the beast in the text, 666, is also the numerical value assigned to the name "Caesar Nero" according to the system of Hebrew numerology. Loyalty to the empire was seen as a direct repudiation of faith in Christ.

It is easy to see how those convinced of their own generation's failings would turn to Revelation as a "proof text" of their position. In the 1970s, for example, Christian activist William Stringfellow compared the times of the Book of Revelation with his contemporary experience of American culture (see his book, *An Ethic for Christians and Other Aliens in a Strange Land*). Stringfellow was neither the first person nor the last to view his era apocalyptically. Those of us today who feel the seduction of the glamour of wealth, the cult of pleasure, and the lure of power laced with violence have some insight into how the apocalyptic worldview might be more contemporary than we care to admit.

By the Numbers

A short course in the significance of numbers (numerology) helps in reading Revelation. The most important key to unlocking the secrets of the book is the number 7—the symbol of fullness and perfection, probably because it is composed of 3 (the indivisible prime number, as in the Trinity) and 4 (the number of completion—think "north, south, east, west" or "earth, wind, fire and water.") Also, the number 7 is significant in many ancient cultures. We see it elsewhere in the Bible in the 7 days of creation, which make the first week; 7 marches around Jericho to bring down the city; 7 ritual washings for cures in Leviticus; 70 times 7 obligations to forgive; and 7 demons expelled from Mary Magdalene, to name a few.

Revelation is addressed to the 7 communities of Asia Minor, a coded reference to the whole Church; 7 messages are delivered to the Church and 7 seals, trumpets and bowls enhance the significance of what's revealed. Look also for less explicit groupings of 7, as in the attributes of the Lamb: power and wealth, wisdom and might, honor and glory and blessing (see 5:12). Although a lamb with 7 horns and 7 eyes might sound repulsive, the image evokes the Lamb's perfection rather than intending a literal description. The number 777, the trinity of perfection attributed to the Lamb, is also the numerical value of "King of Kings, Lord of Lords" in Aramaic.

If the number 7 symbolizes perfection, then the number 6

is imperfection, if not the incarnation of evil. We are not surprised when the number of the beast known as "antichrist" is a trinity of sixes. The beast parodies Jesus in blasphemous ways, bearing 7 heads (a monstrous semblance of perfection) and a mortal wound that has healed, reminiscent of the wounds of the cross. The beast rules for 42 months, an eerie multiplication of 7 and 6.

Other significant numbers are 12 and its multiples. The number 12 was the count of the sons of Jacob and the tribes of Israel thereafter; it was also the number Jesus chose for his Apostles. Those Apostles replaced Judas with Matthias after the resurrection, to preserve the symbolism of the Twelve. Heaven is therefore composed of 24 elders, not to mention 144,000 perfected souls (12 times 12 times 1000, implying multitudes).

Despite its preoccupation with symbolic numbers, the Book of Revelation shows no interest in providing us with an actual calendar of events. From the perspective of Christian apocalypse, the only two important moments in history are the time of Jesus in history and the return of Jesus at the end of history. Every other day on the calendar is insignificant by comparison.

Counterfeit Power vs. Real Authority

When reading the Book of Revelation, we might be forgiven for concluding that the whole thing is about the end of the world and the destruction of sinners. In fact, if you follow the devastation literally, the earth does get destroyed several times over. But the central theme of apocalypse in general—and Revelation in particular—is the matter of *sovereignty*: Who has the power? Is God in charge, or is some other force ruling the world? Most important of all, whom do *you* serve?

Lots of powerful figures rise up over the course of the book. There is "one like the Son of Man" (1:13), a powerful image of Christ borrowed from Daniel 7. He holds seven stars and bears in his mouth the two-edged sword of decision, an image of God's judgment popular in Ezekiel and the prophets. Christ reappears later as the ageless Alpha and the Omega, the gentle Lamb that was slain, the mighty Lion of Judah, the King of

Kings and Lord of Lords, the temple of God, and the lamp of the New Jerusalem.

Contrast those images with the specters of evil that refuse to acknowledge God's sovereignty. First there is the dragon, which threatens harm to the woman holding the promise of the future within her. He does battle with Michael and the archangels, reminiscent of the primordial battle, and we are not surprised when the dragon is identified with those more familiar names, the Devil and Satan. The dragon awaits his henchmen, two beasts that rise from the sea and the earth respectively. These ancient evils remind us of the original chaos that was replaced with the act of creation, when God organized the universe in neat pairs of light and darkness, land and sea, male and female. The goal of the beasts is to reassert primordial chaos in direct opposition to the will of God.

One way of reading Revelation is to see it as a curious replay of the Book of Genesis, sometimes moving forward, sometimes in reverse. As the scrolls are broken open, the power of the Word that created the world is revealed to be still in command, bringing new realities into being as they are spoken. At the same time, Revelation is Genesis played backwards, as the world once so lovingly unfurled, detail by detail, comes to ruin, piece by piece. In the end, creation is rolled up like a worn carpet. Heaven and earth together pass away—and what results is the *new* heaven and the *new* earth, where the justice of God resides at last. Chaos had its first and last stand, but God's order manifested in justice will triumph.

Misuses of Apocalyptic Vision

Because the symbolic imagery of apocalyptic writing is so dense and mysterious, it can easily be misinterpreted. One way it is regularly misused is in the *millennial* movements of the last two thousand years, which seek to identify the precise time of the end of the world. For example, a fellow named William Miller in upstate New York read the book of Revelation in the early 1800s and became convinced that Jesus would return in March 1843. History recalls this event as the "Great Disappointment." The Millerites made new calculations and tried again in October 1844, before the group folded. But one of Miller's disciples, Ellen Gould White, began the Seventh Day Adventists based on a reconfigured idea of the conditions under which Jesus would return—including the embrace of vegetarianism and the refusal of all drugs, from alcohol and cigarettes to medicines. One of her devotees, Dr. John Harvey Kellogg, invented the first breakfast cereal, in part to wean people away from bacon and eggs! Connecting the dots between the cornflake and the Second Coming provides a good example of where the millennial mindset can lead people. The Jehovah's Witnesses, under the direction of Charles Taze Russell, declared near the end of the nineteenth century that Jesus already *had* returned, though invisibly, and that the close of this age would commence in 1914. Millennial thinking is an amazingly unstoppable force.

Theories about the "Rapture" (based on 1 Thessalonians 4:17, Matthew 24, and random verses from prophecy) are likewise tied into apocalyptic worldviews. Rapture belief claims that those who are saved by Christ will also be spared the cataclysmic events of the final days. (The insistence that Christians do not deserve to suffer is intriguing, especially since we follow the God on the cross who promised that what the world did to him, it will surely do to us. Any theology grounded in escaping human suffering seems to me only precariously Christian.)

The most serious misuse of apocalyptic vision in our time, however, is the belief that "holy war" can be justified in its pages. Isn't license given in Revelation to dispatch God's enemies by any means necessary and without compunction or compassion? Isn't the destruction of sinners something God clearly approves of? What such reasoning fails to appreciate is that *God alone* does the dispatching in Revelation. Not one human being raises a sword in all that massive conflict. The message is irrefutable: If there is judging to be done, God will do it; if destruction is to be visited, God will be in charge of delivering the blow. Divine sovereignty needs no help from us in determining who the enemies are or what should be done about them. It is therefore wrong to use apocalyptic literature to defend the idea of waging "holy war."

A Word of Hope

The Book of Revelation may seem an unlikely source of good news, but it is not wrong to think of it as the fifth gospel of the New Testament. Unlike the four Gospels of the Evangelists, this one does not recount the story of Jesus' life and ministry. But like the Gospels, the bottom line of Revelation is that to Christ belongs the victory over sin and death. The good news of Revelation is that God triumphs, Jesus is Lord over all, and the kingdom or reign of God will be ushered in as the fulfillment of God's purposes. These are all primary gospel ideas. They are simply reconsidered through an apocalyptic lens in the Book of Revelation.

Apocalypse *is* good news for people of faith. This world, which has seen its history of pain and terror, will come to an end. The world to come—with its exquisite light, beauty, joy and freedom—will encompass us and have no end. Throughout the most grisly parts of Revelation, even while destruction is raining down on the earth, the possibility of salvation is held out and some embrace it. In fact, *most* do. The detail we often miss is that although a remnant is destroyed each time, the majority are saved in the end. This is significant, because in Hebrew Scripture the persistent theme is the opposite—that only a remnant of the people will be faithful. God punishes the people in the desert so that a remnant may be redeemed. "The faithful remnant" returns to Jerusalem after the exile in Babylon. Even in Romans, Paul speaks of a remnant who will remain true (see Romans 11:5).

Yet in Revelation, it is the remnant—the smaller part—that is lost, and the greater part is redeemed. The reversal speaks volumes: God's desire is to save us, not to lose us. This shifts the point of the book away from "the end of the world" and toward the start of the new one, away from punishment and in the direction of fulfillment. Like the oft-repeated number 7, the Book of Revelation encompasses the hope of creation's fulfillment and not its rejection. From its transcendent perspective, we are given good advice: If you want to know the reason for which you were born, stand with the children of God. God's reign awaits us, now and at the hour of our death, and we can choose to share in that kingdom—not in some arbitrary future final moment, but right now.

Questions for Reflection and Discussion

1. What criteria do you use to make moral decisions? Do you think the Bible tells us precisely what to do in every circumstance of our lives? Explain your answer.

2. What do you believe about afterlife, judgment, and the end of the world? How do your beliefs determine the way you make choices now?

3. Do you think religion should be all positive, or is there room in your faith for negative motivation? How do negative consequences motivate you in other aspects of your life?

4. Name people who wield power and authority over you. Have you ever had to make a choice between civil authority and God's authority? When is patriotism a source of conflict for you?

5. Point to contemporary instances in which the idea of apocalypticism has been misused. How should a Christian respond to "God's enemies," and who determines who those enemies are?

Faith Response

Reflect on those aspects of your life that are at the service of worldly affairs: earning money, providing comforts for the home, saving for the future, looking good in front of others. List the things you do in the service of the reign of God: acts of generosity for the disadvantaged, raising your voice for justice for the powerless, refusing to benefit from systems that oppress others. Compare the two lists, and consider which speaks more eloquently about where your final loyalty lies.

Afterword

The Road of Discipleship

I used to think that "being a Christian" meant "being good." After reflecting on the New Testament for many years, however, I now understand that the goal of being a Christian is to follow Jesus. These two statements might not sound so different at first. But consider the direction each one takes toward its destination.

If being good is the goal, then life is all about us and our efforts. It focuses us on the way of the law, either keeping it or falling short of it. Moral perfection becomes a dreary and thankless task, with its usual companions of guilt, denial and judgmentalism. If, in time, we don't think we're getting better at "being good," we lose heart. (If we *do* think we're getting better at "being good," we're probably kidding ourselves.)

But if following Jesus is our goal, then we are looking in his direction and not back at ourselves. As his followers, we don't have to worry about moral perfection. On the road of discipleship we learn, like Peter did, that Jesus will rescue us when our faith is thin and we start to sink. And just as Paul discovered, Jesus will spin us around and set us in a new direction when we've got God and ourselves all wrong. The road of discipleship can be rough and is not without suffering, as the New Testament makes clear. But along this road we find mercy and forgiveness, two things none of us should leave home without. Although following Jesus most surely will lead to the cross, to God belongs every victory, as John of Patmos revealed in the Book of Revelation. This means, above all, that we do not have to fear our own inadequacy, for the wisdom of the early Church reminds us: "Perfect love casts out fear" (1 John 4:18).

As followers of Jesus, we take up the cry of Peter, "Lord, where else would we go? You alone have the words of everlasting life" (John 6:68). Every other way pales by comparison. In the company of perfect love, we find the courage to dream, to dare, to hope, and to become—at last—the men and women God made us to be.

Appendices

Selected Resources

General Bible Tools

These basic books belong on the bookshelf of every serious student of the Bible.

The New American Bible (National Council of Catholic Bishops)
The New Revised Standard Version Bible (National Council of the Churches of Christ in the U.S.A.)
The New World Dictionary-Concordance to the New American Bible (World Book Publishing)
NRSV Exhaustive Concordance (Thomas Nelson Publishers)
The New Jerome Bible Handbook (Liturgical Press)
Dictionary of the Bible (Simon and Schuster)
Gospel Parallels: A Synopsis of the First Three Gospels (Thomas Nelson Publishers)

Commentaries for Lectionary-Based Scripture Study

The following three resources are for those interested in Bible study in conjunction with the Scripture readings used at Mass. The first two titles follow the Sunday readings. The third title is for those who want to reflect on the daily Mass readings. All are available from Bayard/Twenty-Third Publications.

Alice Camille. *God's Word Is Alive! Entering the Sunday Readings*
——. "Exploring the Sunday Readings." Serial publication mailed monthly
Paul Boudreau. *Between Sundays: Daily Gospel Reflections and Prayers*

Video and Audio Programs

For a better appreciation of how the story of the gospel is retold for each generation, consider the following.

Cotton Patch Gospel. The story of Jesus set in present-day Georgia. Score by Harry Chapin. 110 min.

The Evangelists Speak for Themselves. Original dramatizations by Fr. William Burke of each of the four Evangelists appearing before a contemporary audience to explain his individual Gospel. Three 45-75 minute video tapes. (ACTA Publications)

Godspell. Based on the Broadway musical and Matthew's Gospel. 105 min.

The Gospel According to Matthew [Italian with subtitles]. Director Paolo Pasolini's bracing masterpiece uses only the text of the Gospel. 136 min.

Gospel Food for Hungry Christians. Live presentations recorded by theologian and master storyteller John Shea on each of the four gospels. Six 60-90 minute audio tapes each set. (ACTA Publications)

Jesus Christ Superstar. Rock opera filmed on location in Israel. 108 min.

Peter and Paul. An intriguing retelling of episodes from Acts that incorporates portions of the epistles. Featuring Anthony Hopkins and Robert Foxworth. 194 min.

Special New Testament Topics

All of these fine books on the New Testament are available from Liturgical Press.

Wilfrid Harrington, OP. *The Jesus Story*
Carl R. Kazmierski. *John the Baptist: Prophet and Evangelist*
Earl Richard, ed. *New Views on Luke and Acts*
Raymond F. Collins. *John and His Witness*
Hubert Richards. *The Gospel According to St. Paul*
Florence M. Gillman. *Women Who Knew Paul*
William J. Dalton, SJ. *Galatians Without Tears*
Rea McDonnell, SSND. *The Catholic Epistles and Hebrews*
Adela Yarbro Collins. *The Apocalypse*
Charles Homer Giblin, SJ. *The Book of Revelation: The Open Book of Prophecy*

New Testament Books of the Bible

The following is the standard listing of books in the New Testament appearing in the order used in most contemporary Catholic and Protestant Bibles.

Matthew
Mark
Luke
John
The Acts of the Apostles
The Letter to the Romans
The First Letter to the Corinthians
The Second Letter to the Corinthians
The Letter to the Galatians
The Letter to the Ephesians
The Letter to the Philippians
The Letter to the Colossians
The First Letter to the Thessalonians
The Second Letter to the Thessalonians
The First Letter to Timothy
The Second Letter to Timothy
The Letter to Titus
The Letter to Philemon
The Letter to the Hebrews
The Letter of James
The First Letter of Peter
The Second Letter of Peter
The First Letter of John
The Second Letter of John
The Third Letter of John
The Letter of Jude
The Book of Revelation

Approximate Dates of Key Events in the New Testament

Bible resources vary on these estimates, so use them as guide-posts only:

6-4 B.C. Estimates for the birth of Jesus born at the end of the reign of King Herod the Great (ruled 37-4 B.C.)

28-29 A.D. Start of Jesus' ministry, in relationship to the reign of the Roman emperor Tiberius (ruled 14-37)

29 Arrest of John the Baptist

30-33 Jesus' last days in Jerusalem (John's Gospel posits a one-year ministry; the Synoptic tradition presumes three years), intersecting with former high priest Annas (served 6-15) and present high priest Caiaphas (served 18-36) and Roman prefect of Judea Pontius Pilate (governed 26-36)

35 Death of first martyr Stephen

36-37 Conversion of Paul of Tarsus at Damascus

42 James, son of Zebedee and brother to John, first Apostle martyred by King Herod Agrippa

46-49 Paul's first missionary journey

49 Council of Jerusalem exempts Gentiles from Mosaic law

50-52 Paul's second missionary journey

54-58 Paul's third missionary journey, ending in his arrest

60-63 Paul appeals to Caesar, journeys to Rome, and is kept under house arrest

63-67 Estimates for martyrdom of Peter

64-68 Estimates for martyrdom of Paul

70 Destruction of the Jerusalem Temple by the Romans

81-96 Persecution of the Christians by Domitian

85-90 Reconstruction of Jewish faith by Pharisees at Jamnia

A Likely Chronological Ordering of the Writing of the New Testament

Those who hold to the literal authorship of each of these documents (i.e., that Paul wrote all thirteen letters attributed to him, and Peter wrote his, etc.) will find these dates less helpful. Scholars debate them heatedly. They are intended as one possible organization, and all dates are approximate.

51 A.D.	1 Thessalonians
54	Galatians
57	1, 2 Corinthians; Philemon; Philippians
58	Romans
61-63	2 Thessalonians, Colossians, Ephesians
60-70	Gospel of Mark
80-90	Gospel of Matthew, Gospel of Luke, Acts of the Apostles, and Hebrews
90-100	Gospel of John; 1, 2 Timothy; Titus; 1 Peter; James; Jude; 1, 2, 3 John; Revelation
100-140	2 Peter

Important Dates in the Formation of the Bible We Have Today

100 A.D.   Jewish canon of Scripture established (this becomes our "Old Testament")

367   Athanasius lists the New Testament canon

382-405   Jerome compiles the Vulgate translation in Latin

1228   Stephen Langton, archbishop of Paris, numbers the chapters of each book of the Bible

c. 1455   John Gutenberg prints first mass-produced bibles

1545-1563   Council of Trent reestablishes the complete canon of Scripture, including the Deuterocanonical books deleted by Protestant reformers

1555   Robert Etienne fixes the number of Bible verses

1609-1763   Douay-Rheims translation and revision of the Bible made from the Vulgate for Catholic use in English (King James Version released in 1611)

1943   Pope Pius XII, *Divino Afflante Spiritu,* considers how culture shapes the writing and understanding of Scripture

1947-1956   Dead Sea Scroll discovery transforms Biblical scholarship

1965   Vatican II, *Dogmatic Constitution on Divine Revelation,* encourages contemporary understanding of Scripture

1970   New American Bible, first Catholic Bible translated from the original languages since the Vulgate by Jerome

1990   New Revised Standard Version Bible, first ecumenical, English-language Bible approved for use by Protestants, Catholics and Eastern Orthodox

Also from ACTA Publications

Invitation to the Old Testament
A Catholic Approach to the Hebrew Scriptures
Alice Camille
A companion to *Invitation to the New Testament,* providing an overview of the entire Old Testament through the lens of Catholic tradition and teaching. (112-page softcover, $9.95)

Invitation to Catholicism
Beliefs + Teachings + Practices
Alice Camille
Everyone from lifelong Catholics to interested non-Catholics will welcome the easy-to-understand, logical explanations found in this overview of Catholic beliefs, teachings and practices. (240-page softcover, $9.95)

Getting to Know the Bible
An Introduction to Sacred Scripture for Catholics
Rev. Melvin L. Farrell, SS
revised by Joseph McHugh
A clear, concise overview of the entire Bible for Catholics, offering an introduction to all the major books of Scripture, from Genesis through Revelation. (112-page softcover, $6.95)

The Rosary
Mysteries of Joy, Light, Sorrow and Glory
Alice Camille
New reflections on each of the mysteries of the Rosary, including the new Mysteries of Light, with a concise history of the Rosary and reflections on its meaning for the new millennium. (112-page softcover, $6.95)

Life in Christ
A Catholic Catechism for Adults
Revs. Gerard Weber and James Killgallon
This bestselling catechism for adults presents all aspects of Catholic teaching in a question-and-answer format that is easy to use yet thorough and comprehensive. (327-page softcover, $6.95)

Available from booksellers or call 800-397-2282
www.actapublications.com